S0-BNS-844

Study Guide
Volume 2, Chapters 15-26

for use with

Financial & Managerial Accounting

Fourteenth Edition

Jan R. Williams
University of Tennessee

Susan F. Haka
Michigan State University

Mark S. Bettner
Bucknell University

Joseph Carcello
University of Tennessee

McGraw-Hill Irwin

Boston   Burr Ridge, IL   Dubuque, IA   Madison, WI   New York   San Francisco   St. Louis
Bangkok   Bogotá   Caracas   Kuala Lumpur   Lisbon   London   Madrid   Mexico City
Milan   Montreal   New Delhi   Santiago   Seoul   Singapore   Sydney   Taipei   Toronto

McGraw-Hill
Irwin

Study Guide Volume 2, Chapters 15-26 for use with
FINANACIAL & MANAGERIAL ACCOUNTING
Jan R. Williams, Susan F. Haka, Mark S. Bettner, Joseph Carcello

Published by McGraw-Hill/Irwin, an imprint of The McGraw-Hill Companies, Inc., 1221 Avenue of the Americas, New York, NY 10020. Copyright © 2008 by The McGraw-Hill Companies, Inc. All rights reserved.

No part of this publication may be reproduced or distributed in any form or by any means, or stored in a database or retrieval system, without the prior written consent of The McGraw-Hill Companies, Inc., including, but not limited to, in any network or other electronic storage or transmission, or broadcast for distance learning.

1 2 3 4 5 6 7 8 9 0 QPD/QPD 0 9 8 7 6

ISBN   978-0-07-326816-3
MHID   0-07-326816-X

www.mhhe.com

The McGraw-Hill Companies

Table of Contents

GLOBAL BUSINESS AND ACCOUNTING

Highlights of the Chapter

1.   *Globalization* is a process by which managers become aware of the impact of international activities on their company's future. Globalization activities typically progress through a series of outward growth stages that include exporting, licensing, joint ventures, wholly owned subsidiaries, and global sourcing.

2.   *Exporting*, at the simplest level, is selling a good or service to a foreign customer. Exporting enables the producing company to maintain control over product creation. Licensing, in contrast, gives up some control for a monetary return. *International licensing* is a contractual agreement between a company and a foreign party allowing the use of trademarks, patents, technology, etc. Many international companies are involved in some form of international product licensing. *International joint ventures*, are companies created by two or more companies from different countries, whereas *wholly owned international* subsidiaries are created when a single company purchases 100% equity control of another company in a different country. *Global sourcing* requires the coordination of numerous business activities, across international boundaries, and typically involves a combination of exporting, licensing, joint ventures, and wholly owned subsidiaries.

3.   The strategic direction of planned globalization has implications for the type of accounting information gathered, created, and reported. For example, the type of information gathered and reported for a wholly owned international subsidiary must be more detailed and control oriented than the information required to monitor exporting and licensing activities.

4.   Four related environmental forces shape globalization. They are: (1) political and legal systems, (2) economic systems, (3) culture, and (4) technology and infrastructure.

5.   *Political risk* often occurs when governments take ownership or control over business assets and operations. When a foreign country nationalizes its industries, for example, companies must often give up ownership of their assets to the controlling country's government. Government may also intervene in business activities by enacting restrictive laws pertaining to taxes, licensing fees, or tariffs. Governments often create tariffs, duties, and special trade zones to encourage or discourage particular types of importing or exporting activities.

6.   *Legal reporting* requirements vary significantly from country to country. Differences in accounting practices reflect the influences that shape business activity in a country, its legal environment, and the primary providers of capital for businesses. For example, in the United States, legal reporting requirements are based primarily on the need to provide information to private investors and creditors. In those countries where private capital is unavailable, reporting requirements are often oriented toward the needs of centralized government planning.

7.   Differences in accounting and reporting practices among countries create problems in trying to analyze and compare accounting information. As long as a company operates solely within its own borders, differences in financial reporting practices are not as significant as they are if business activity extends across borders.

8.   Reporting differences also present problems for companies that sell their securities in foreign markets. *Cross-border financing* activities have led to an interest in the *harmonization of accounting standards*, a phrase used to describe the standardization of accounting methods and principles throughout the world.

9. The ***International Accounting Standards Committee*** (IASC) is particularly interested in harmonization and is charged with the responsibility of establishing and gaining acceptance of international accounting standards.

10. The economic systems under which businesses operate significantly affect the form and availability of accounting information. In a ***planned economy***, the government uses central planning to allocate resources and determine and output among various economic segments. In ***market economies,*** ownership of land and the means of production are private, and the market dictates the allocation of resources and the output among segments of the economy.

11. The way businesses are organized into industrial organizations contributes to differences in how capital is raised around the globe. In some Asian countries, for example, companies group themselves into conglomerates representing different industries. Within these cartels of companies, suppliers receive loans, investment capital, technology, and long-term supply agreements from customers. In the United States, antitrust and price-fixing laws often preclude these types of business relationships.

12. ***Culture*** may be thought of as the way in which individuals act and perceive each other's actions. U.S. cultural practices have significant affects on the way foreign companies conduct business in the United States. Likewise, many commonly accepted U. S. business practices would not be acceptable in other cultures.

13. Experts on culture have identified several variables that differ among international locations. Of the cultural differences identified, the variables with the most significant implications for management accounting and production include: (1) Individualism versus collectivism, (2) Uncertainty avoidance, (3) Short-versus long-term orientation, and (4) Large versus small power distance.

14. ***Individualism versus collectivism*** refers to the interdependence among individuals in a society or culture. High interdependence among individuals connotes collectivism, whereas low interdependence is connotes individualism.

15. ***Uncertainty avoidance*** refers to the extent to which members of a society or culture feel uncomfortable or threatened by unknown or uncertain situations.

16. ***Short-versus long-term orientation*** refers to the extent to which a society or culture values lasting relationships, social order, and personal stability.

17. ***Large versus small power distance*** refers to the extent to which a society or culture adheres to the idea that everyone is created equal and should have an equal voice.

18. Cultural differences pose problems regarding the design and administration of accounting systems. A budgeting system that is effective in one culture may be completely ineffective in another. Even within one culture or country, there are highly diverse groups in terms of religion, ethnic groups, language, and income level. These differences also have implications for effective business management.

19. Training and educational differences complicate cultural differences through variation in the infrastructure, educational level, and ability to transfer information and knowledge between and among various geographic locations and peoples. These differences create barriers to successful international business operations. Companies that create joint ventures or acquire wholly owned subsidiaries often find few employees with the education and technical training available in the U. S. workforce.

20. ***Infrastructure impediments*** also pose problems for globalization. Poor access to communications equipment, inadequate transportation systems, and unreliable power sources make establishing international business in some locations difficult.

21. In addition to environmental characteristics, companies with international business dealings also encounter problems from multiple securities and the exchange rates related to each. A currency

exchange rate is the amount it costs to purchase one unit of currency with another currency. Thus, the exchange rate may be viewed as the price of buying one unit of foreign currency, as stated in terms of the domestic currency (which, for our purpose, is U. S. dollars).

22. Exchange rates may be used to determine how much of one currency is equivalent to a given amount of another currency. The process of restating an amount of foreign currency in terms of the equivalent number of dollars is called *translating* the foreign currency.

23. In the financial press, currencies are often described as strong or weak, or as rising or falling against another. A currency is described as strong when its exchange rate is falling. Exchange rates fluctuate due to changes in the environmental forces discussed earlier.

24. When a U. S. Company buys or sells merchandise in a transaction with a foreign company, the transaction can be stated in terms of dollars or in terms of the foreign currency. If the price of merchandise bought or sold is stated in terms of dollars, the U. S. company encounters no special accounting problems. Such is not the case if the transaction is stated in terms of the foreign currency.

25. If the transaction price is stated in terms of the foreign currency, the U. S. company encounters two problems. First, the transaction must be *translated* into dollars before the transaction can be recorded. Second, a problem arises if the purchase or sale is made on account, and the exchange rate *changes*, between the date of the transaction and the date that the account is paid or received. This fluctuation in exchange rates will cause the U. S. company to experience either a *gain* or *loss* in the settlement of the transaction.

26. Having an *account payable* that must be paid in a foreign currency results in a gain for the U. S. company if the exchange rate declines between the date of the transaction and the date of payment. A gain results because fewer dollars are needed to repay the debt than had originally been owed. An increase in the exchange rate causes the U. S. company to incur a loss because more dollars must be spent than originally owed in order to purchase the foreign currency needed to settle the account payable. U. S. companies that *import* foreign products often have large liabilities (accounts payable) that are fixed in terms of the foreign currency that must eventually be paid to settle the account.

27. Having an *account receivable* that will be collected in a foreign currency results in a loss for the U. S. company if the exchange rate declines between the date of transaction and the date of payment. A loss results because the amount of foreign currency collected in a settlement of the receivable will convert to fewer U. S. dollars than it would have on the day that the transaction originally transpired. An increase in the exchange rate results in a gain for the U. S. company because the amount of foreign currency collected in settlement of the receivable will convert into more U. S. dollars than it would have on the day that the transaction originally transpired. U. S. companies that *export* products to foreign countries often have large receivables that are fixed in terms of the foreign currency that will eventually be collected to settle the account.

28. Gains and losses resulting from exchange rate fluctuations are normally recorded at the time the related payable or receivable is settled. An exception to this practice occurs at the end of each accounting period. An *adjusting entry* is required at the end of each accounting period to recognize gains or losses that have accumulated on foreign payables and receivables through the balance sheet date. These gains and losses are included in the income statement where they typically follow income from operations. They are presented in a manner much like interest expense and gains and losses on the sale of plant assets.

29. There are two basic approaches to avoiding losses from fluctuations in foreign exchange rates. One approach is to insist that receivables and payables be settled in terms of specified amounts of domestic currency. The other approach is called hedging.

30. *Hedging* is the strategy of taking off-setting positions in a foreign currency to avoid losses from fluctuations in foreign exchange rates. A company that has similar amounts of accounts

receivable and accounts payable in the same foreign currency automatically has hedged position. A company that does not have similar dollar amounts of payable and receivables in the same foreign currency may create a hedged position by buying or selling *future contracts*, or *futures*.

31. A future contract is, in effect, an account receivable in foreign currency. A company with only foreign payables may hedge its position by *purchasing* a similar dollar amount of foreign currency future contracts. A company with only foreign receivables would hedge its position by *selling* future contracts, i.e., creating an offsetting liability payable in foreign currency.

32. Many corporations have subsidiaries organized and operating in foreign countries. These foreign subsidiaries should be included in the parent company's consolidated financial statements. Several complex technical issues are involved in preparing consolidated statements that include foreign subsidiaries. First, the accounting records of the subsidiary must be translated into U. S. dollars. Next, the accounting principles in use in the foreign country may differ from the generally accepted accounting principles (GAAP) used in the United States.

33. Readers of the financial statements of a U. S. corporation need not be concerned with these technical problems. Once accountants have completed the consolidation process, the consolidated financial statements are expressed in U. S. dollars and conform to the GAAP used in the United States.

34. Differences in exchange rates can create significant complexities for firms practicing global sourcing. These firms must estimate costs that will be incurred in multiple countries involved in producing the merchandise to be sold in the open market. The costs associated with various phases of production (including the cost of labor, materials, and shipping) are often stated in terms of different foreign currencies. Making accurate estimates of costs in a global value chain is one of the biggest challenges facing a company wishing to become more global.

35. In many countries, product costs also include expenses incurred to expedite official paperwork. In many countries, bribery is also a part of doing business and is not considered wrong or unethical. The Foreign Corrupt Practices Act (FCPA) prescribes fines and jail time for American managers violating its rules. The FCPA has implications for accounting in two specific areas: record keeping and internal control procedures.

TEST YOURSELF ON GLOBAL BUSINESS AND ACCOUNTING

True or False

For each of the following statements, circle the T or the F to indicate whether the statement is true or false.

T F   1. Globalization typically progresses through a series of stages that include legal reporting, foreign currency transactions, and cultural sensitivity.

T F   2. In the United States, banks provide most of the capital for international businesses.

T F   3. In a planned economy, the government uses central planning to allocate resources and determine output among various industrial segments.

T F   4. Culturally speaking, the industrial organization of Asian countries is characterized by individualism.

T F   5. The International Accounting Standards Committee develops accounting standards that must be followed by all multinational companies.

T F 6. An American company that buys from (or sells to) a foreign company may have gains and losses from fluctuations in currency exchange rates even if the American company does not have a foreign subsidiary.

T F 7. Restating an amount of foreign currency in terms of the equivalent number of units of domestic currency is termed *translating* the foreign currency.

T F 8. The *exchange rate*, for a foreign currency will fluctuate if the worldwide supply of currency exceeds demand.

T F 9. If the U. S. dollar is strengthening in the world currency markets, an American company with large accounts payable due in specified amounts of foreign currencies will experience losses from exchange rate fluctuations.

T F 10. If the exchange rate for a particular foreign currency is rising, an American company with receivables in this currency will recognize gains from the exchange rate fluctuations.

T F 11. Large imports but small exports tend to weaken a country's currency.

T F 12. High interest rates relative to the rate of inflation tend to weaken a country's currency.

T F 13. The balance sheet of a multinational corporation has multiple money columns, showing the financial statement amounts in various currencies, such as dollars, yen, and pounds.

T F 14. The accounting standards and principles used in the preparation of financial statements vary from one country to another.

T F 15. A multinational corporation headquartered in the United States prepares consolidated financial statements which include its foreign subsidiaries and which comply with generally accepted accounting principles.

Completion Statements

Fill in the necessary word to complete the following statements:

1. _____ is the process of managers becoming aware of the impact of international activities on the future of their company.

2. In _____ _____, ownership of land and the means of production are private, and markets dictate the allocation of resources and the output among segments of the economy.

3. The mental mindset that affects the way individuals in a society act and perceive each other's actions may be viewed as a society's _____.

4. The close coordination of R & D, manufacturing, and marketing across national boundaries is typically referred to as _____ _____.

5.   The _____ _____ _____ _____ is responsible for developing international accounting standards.

6.   The process of restating an amount of foreign currency in terms of the equivalent number of U. S. dollars is termed _____ the foreign currency.

7.   Assume that an American company purchases merchandise on account from a Japanese company at a price of ¥500,000. At the date of this purchase, the exchange rate is $.0106. The American company should record a liability of $_____.

8.   Assume that the exchange rate for the British pound is falling relative to the U. S. dollar. American companies making credit sales to British companies will experience (gains, losses) _____ and American companies making credit purchases from British companies will experience (gains, losses) _____ as a result of the fluctuations in the exchange rate.

9.   Assume that an American company incurs a liability for 100,000 French francs when the exchange rate is $0.1900 per franc, and that the company pays off this liability when the exchange rate is $0.2000 per franc. The company will report a (gain, loss) _____ of $_____ from the fluctuation in the exchange rate.

10.   An American exporter with substantial amounts of contracts stated in a foreign currency may avoid loses from fluctuations in foreign exchange rates by _____ future contracts. This strategy of holding offsetting positions in the foreign currency is called _____.

Multiple Choice

Choose the best answer for each of the following questions and enter the identifying letter in the space provided.

___ 1. Globalization typically progresses through a series of stages. The first stage of globalization often involves:
   a.   Exporting.

   b.   International joint ventures.

   c.   Wholly owned international subsidiaries.

   d.   International licensing.

___ 2. Which of the following is *not* an environmental force affecting how accounting information is measured, reported, and created?
   a.   Political and legal systems.

   b.   Global sourcing.

   c.   Economic systems.

   d.   Culture.

_ 3.   The extent to which members of a society feel uncomfortable or threatened by unknown or uncertain situations is sometimes referred to as:

    a.   Power distance.

    b.   Long-term orientation.

    c.   Collectivism.

    d.   Uncertainty avoidance.

_ 4.   Fashion House, an American company, purchases merchandise on account from a French company at a price of 40,000 French francs. Payment is due in 90 days and the current exchange rate is $.1900 per French franc. On the date of this purchase, Fashion House should:

    a.   Record a liability of 40,000 French francs.

    b.   Record a liability of $7,600.

    c.   Record a liability of $235,294.

    d.   Disclose the obligation in a footnote to the financial statements, as the amount of the liability cannot be determined with certainty until the exchange rate at the payment date is known.

_ 5.   In the evening news, a newscaster made the following statement: "Today a weak U. S. dollar fell sharply against the German deutsche mark, but rose slightly against the British pound." This statement indicates that today:

    a.   The exchange rate for the deutsche mark, stated in dollars, is falling.

    b.   The exchange rate for the pound, stated in dollars, is rising.

    c.   The pound was a weaker currency than the dollar.

    d.   The pound was a stronger currency than the deutsche mark.

_ 6.   European Look purchased cashmere sweaters from England on account at a price of £10,000. On the purchase date the exchange rate was $1.61 per British pound, but when European Look paid the liability the exchange rate was $1.58 per pound. When this foreign account payable is paid. European Look should record a:

    a.   Liability of $300.

    b.   Loss of $300.

    c.   Receivable of $300.

    d.   Gain of $300.

_ 7.   Assume that the exchange rate for the British pound is rising relative to the U. S. dollar. An American company will incur *losses* from this rising exchange rate if the company is making:

    a.   Credit sales to British companies at prices stated in pounds.

    b.   Credit purchases from British companies with prices stated in U. S. dollars.

    c.   Credit sales to British companies at prices stated in U. S. dollars.

    d.   Credit purchases from British companies at prices stated in pounds.

8. Assume that the exchange rate for the German deutsche mark is *falling* relative to the U. S. dollar. An American company will incur *losses* from this falling exchange rate if it is making:

a. Credit sales to German companies at prices stated in deutsche marks.

b. Credit purchases from German companies at prices stated in U. S. dollars.

c. Credit sales to German companies at prices stated in U. S. dollars.

d. Credit purchases from German companies at prices stated in deutsche marks.

Exercises

1. Listed below are eight technical accounting terms emphasized in this chapter.

Multinational company	**"Strong" currency**
"Weak" currency	**Translating**
International accounting	**Foreign currency**
Exchange rate	**Gain on fluctuations in foreign exchange rates**

Each of the following statements may (or may not) describe one of these technical terms. In the space provided below each statement, indicate the accounting term described, or answer "None" if the statement does not correctly describe any of the terms.

a. A business that is organized and operating in a different country from its parent company.

_____

b. The process of restating an amount of foreign currency in terms of the domestic currency (dollars).

_____

c. Any unit of foreign currency worth more than one U. S. dollar.

_____

d. The ratio at which one currency may be converted into another.

_____

e. A condition of the domestic currency that helps companies that sell domestically produced products, either at home or abroad.

_____

f. Accounting for business activities that span national borders.

_____

g. A currency whose exchange rate is rising relative to that of most other currencies.

_____

2. Translate the following amounts of foreign currency into an equivalent number of U. S. dollars using the exchange rates in the table shown below.

Country	Currency	Exchange Rate
Britain	Pound (£)	$1.6295
France	French franc (FF)	.1991
Japan	Yen (¥)	.0106
Mexico	Peso ($)	.1586
Germany	Deutsche mark (DM)	.7022

a. DM15,000
b. £130,000
c. ¥300,000

3. Jill Adams owns a company that imports perfume from France. In the space provided, prepare journal entries to record the following events.

Nov. 24   Purchased perfume from St. Jean, a French company, at a price of 50,000 francs, due in 60 days. The current exchange rate is $.1913 per franc. (Adams uses the perpetual inventory method.)

Dec. 21   Adams made a year-end adjusting entry relating to the account payable to St. Jean. The exchange rate at year-end was $.1900 per franc.

Jan. 23   Issued a check for $9,540 (U. S. dollars) to Global Bank in full settlement of the liability to St. Jean. the current exchange rate is $.1908 per franc.

3.

	General Journal		
Nov. 24	Inventory		
Dec. 31			
2005			
Jan. 23			

SOLUTIONS TO CHAPTER 15 SELF-TEST

True or False

1. **F** Globalization typically progresses through a series of stages that include exporting, licensing, joint ventures, wholly owned subsidiaries, and global sourcing.

2. **F** In the United States, most large international companies raise capital by selling their securities in well-developed capital markets.

3. **T** In a planned economy, land and production facilities are government owned and controlled. The former Soviet Union and the Soviet Eastern Bloc countries used central planning and had planned economies. China continues to use central planning extensively.

4. **F** Asian countries, such as South Korea and Japan, have collectivist types of industrial organization. Studies have shown that collectivist cultures place less emphasis upon the importance of control in business organizations.

5. **F** The international Accounting Standards Committee has no enforcement power.

6. **T** Whenever an American company buys or sells merchandise in a *credit* transaction with a foreign company, and the contract price is stipulated in the *foreign currency*, any fluctuations in the exchange rate will cause gains and losses.

7. **T** Exchange rates are used to determine how much of one currency is equivalent to a given amount of another currency.

8. **T** Exchange rates (the "price" of one currency stated in terms of another) fluctuate based upon supply and demand.

9. **F** A *gain* results because fewer dollars are needed to repay the debt (stipulated in a foreign currency) than when the debt arose.

10. **T** An increase in the exchange rate causes a creditor to incur a gain on receivables in that currency, and a debtor to incur a loss on payables stipulated in that currency.

11. **T** With small exports, there is not a great demand by purchasers for the country's currency to pay for the goods exported. Low demand causes the exchange rate to decline relative to other countries' currencies.

12. **F** When a politically stable country offers high interest rates relative to inflation, foreign investors will want to invest funds in that country. To do this, they must obtain that country's currency; high demand strengthens a country's currency.

13. **F** A company's financial statements are presented in one currency; financial statement amounts for foreign subsidiaries are translated into that currency.

14. **T** Generally accepted accounting principles used in America are *not* in worldwide use.

15. **T** In addition to translating the accounting records of foreign subsidiaries to U. S. dollars, the parent company must adjust a foreign subsidiary's accounting records to U. S. GAAP.

Completion Statements

1. Globalization. 2. Market economies. 3. Culture. 4. Global sourcing. 5. International Accounting Standards Committee. 6. Translating. 7. $5,300. 8. Losses, gains. 9. Loss; $1,000. 10. Selling, hedging.

Multiple Choice

1. Answer **a** – Most companies begin globalization by exporting goods to foreign customers. While exporting maintains control over production, international licensing is a more complex relationship which gives up control for a monetary return. International joint ventures and wholly owned international subsidiaries are usually an outgrowth of exporting and licensing activities.

2. Answer **b** – Global sourcing is the close coordination of diverse business activities across international boundaries. Global sourcing represents the degree to which a company is engaged in globalization. It does not represent an environmental force. Economic systems, culture, technology, infrastructure, and political and legal systems are considered environmental forces which influence the way in which accounting is measured, reported, and created.

3. Answer **d** – Uncertainty avoidance is a to describe people's comfort in dealing with ambiguous situations. Power distance refers to perceptions regarding the distribution of power within and across institutions and organizations. Long-term orientations are associated with valuing highly perseverance, thriftiness, maintaining order, and lasting relationships. Collectivism refers to a high interdependence among members of a particular culture.

4. Answer **b** – (40,000FF x $.1900 per franc = $7,600). Answer **d** is incorrect; the amount of the liability **is known** as the purchase date. Any changes in the amount of this liability will be **future** events and will be recorded if and when they occur.

5. Answer **c** – if the dollar "rose slightly" against the pound, the exchange rate for the pound (stated in dollars) has declines. Thus, the pound was a weaker currency than the dollar.

6. Answer **d** – European Look's liability to the English company originally was $16,100 (£10,000 x $1.61 per pound). However, European Look ultimately paid only $15,800 to settle this liability (£10,000 x $1.58 per pound), thus resulting in a $300 gain from the fluctuation in the exchange rate.

7. Answer **d** – as a result of the rising exchange rate, the American company will have to pay **more dollars** to settle its liability (for a fixed number of pounds) at the settlement date than was required earlier, at the date of the initial purchase. This difference is a **loss** from exchange rate fluctuations. Answer **a** is incorrect, because the seller's receivable (which is fixed in pounds) becomes equivalent to more dollars as the exchange rate for the pound rises. Answers **b** and **c** are incorrect; if the receivables or payables are fixed in dollars, the American company will experience neither a gain nor a loss from exchange rate fluctuations.

8. Answer **a** – if the exchange rate for the deutsche mark is falling, an American company with receivables of a fixed number of deutsche marks is seeing the value of this asset decline.

Solutions to Exercises

1.
   a. None (The statement describes a **foreign subsidiary**; a multinational company is one that does business in more than one country.)
   b. Translating
   c. None (The terms **strong currency** and **weak currency** refer to the direction of recent changes in the exchange rate, not to the absolute level of this rate.)
   d. Exchange rate
   e. "Weak" currency
   f. International accounting
   g. "Strong" currency

2.

    a. $10,533 (DM 15,000 x $.7022 per deutsche mark.)

    b. $211,835 (£130,000 x $1.6295 per pound)

    c. $3,180 (¥300,000 x $.0106 per yen)

3.

General Journal			
Nov. 24	Inventory	9,565	
	Accounts Payable – St. Jean		9,565
	Purchased perfume from St. Jean for 50,000 francs, exchange		
	rate, $.1913 per franc (50,000FF x $.1913 = $9,565)		
Dec. 31	Accounts Payable – St. Jean	65	
	Gain on Fluctuation in Foreign Exchange Rates		65
	To adjust liability to St. Jean based on year-end exchange rate:		
	Original balance $9,565		
	Adjusted balance (50,000FF x $.1900) $9,500		
	Gain through year-end $ 65		
2005			
Jan. 23	Accounts Payable – St. Jean	9,500	
	Loss on Fluctuation in Foreign Exchange Rates	40	
	Cash		9,540
	Paid 50,000 franc liability to St. Jean; exchange rate,		
	$.1908 per franc (50,000FF x $.1908 = $9,540)		

16

MANAGEMENT ACCOUNTING: A BUSINESS PARTNER

Highlights of the Chapter

1. Management accounting is the design and use of accounting information systems inside the firm to achieve the firm's objectives. Management accounting reports are not governed by generally accepted accounting principles or by tax regulations. Therefore, they can be uniquely prepared and presented to best suit the needs of individual managers.

2. Management accounting information is important to anyone functioning in a managerial capacity. An understanding of basic management accounting principles can benefit theater managers, football team owners, city planners, park and recreation directors, etc.

3. Three principles govern how management accounting systems are designed. First, management accounting systems help to decide who has decision-making authority over company assets. Second, accounting information produced by or created from the management accounting system supports planning and decision making. Finally, management accounting reports provide a means of monitoring, evaluating and rewarding performance.

4. To achieve organizational goals, managers are assigned decision-making authority for some of the firm's assets. Employees within an organization know their decision-making responsibilities because they are outlined in a variety of ways, such as in job descriptions, verbal instructions, and through management accounting documents and reports.

5. Managers need reliable and timely information on which to base their decisions. They need information oriented toward both their specific operations and toward other parts of the organization's value chain. A *value chain* is the linked set of activities and resources necessary to create and deliver products or services to customers. Plant managers, for example, require information from other parts of the value chain such as engineering and sales. They also need information from both internal operations and externally oriented benchmark sources.

6. More and more organizations are sharing information. It is very common for organizations to participate in and undertake *benchmark studies*. Independent consultants often create benchmark reports by collecting information for multiple companies in the same industry. These studies show an organization how its costs and processes compare to others in the same industry.

7. Organizations also share information with customers and suppliers in their value chain. For example, in order for shipments from suppliers to arrive at the exact time they are needed for use in production, buyers and suppliers share their production information. Customers often require or are voluntarily provided product quality and or safety information. Management accounting systems provide a wide range of information for users inside and outside of the firm.

8. The assets over which managers have decisions-making authority do not belong to them personally. The corporation owns these assets, and profits earned from these assets belong to the corporation. To make certain that assets are generating adequate profits, corporations monitor the outcomes of the decisions made by managers. When the corporation is owned by many shareholders, the external financial statements serve this monitoring role for the corporation as a whole. Parallel monitoring systems are designed to serve similar functions inside corporations. Frequently, managerial rewards and bonuses are related to the information contained in these internally prepared financial documents.

9. Creating accounting information systems that can satisfy the demands of both external users (shareholders, creditors, IRS, SEC) and internal users (plant managers, marketing managers, human resources personnel, CFO's, CEO's) is very challenging.

10. Do to rapidly evolving changes in technology and information needs of business managers, the study of management accounting is required throughout one's professional career.

11. In a manufacturing company, product costs are of vital importance to both managerial and financial accountants. Managerial accountants must supply managers with prompt and reliable information about manufacturing costs for decision purposes, whereas financial accountants need this information in order to report inventory and cost of goods sold figures to investors and creditors.

12. In a merchandising company, the cost of goods sold is based upon the cost of *purchasing* merchandise for resale. In a manufacturing company, cost of goods sold represents the various costs of *manufacturing* the products sold.

13. A typical manufacturer buys raw materials and converts them into finished products. Manufacturing costs associated with this process may be divided into three broad categories:

    a. *Direct materials* – the cost of raw materials and component parts that are directly traceable to manufactured products.

    b. *Direct labor* – wages and other payroll costs relating to employees whose efforts are directly traceable to manufactured products.

    c. *Manufacturing overhead* – a "catch all" classification which includes all manufacturing costs other than direct materials and direct labor.

14. Manufacturing costs are the costs of creating inventory and are termed *inventoriable costs* or *product costs*. Such costs are associated with manufacturing inventory available for sale. Thus, until goods are sold, product costs represent inventory, which is an asset. As inventory is sold, related product costs are deducted from revenue as the cost of goods sold. This process is an example of the *matching principle*, the concept that revenue should be offset by the costs incurred in generating that revenue.

15. Unlike manufacturing costs, *period costs* are associated with time periods instead of products. As such, period costs are charged directly to expense accounts as opposed to inventory accounts. These accounts include selling expenses, general and administrative expenses, interest expense, and income tax expenses.

16. Manufacturing companies normally have three distinct types of inventories:

    a. *Materials inventory* – direct materials on hand for use in the manufacturing process.

    b. *Work in process inventory* – partially completed goods upon which production activities have been started but are not yet completed.

    c. *Finished goods inventory* – finished product available for sale to customers. All three of these inventories are shown at their cost and are classified as current assets in the balance sheet. The cost of the materials inventory is based upon its purchase price; the cost of the work in process inventory and the finished goods inventory is based upon the manufacturing costs incurred in producing these units.

17. When a *perpetual* inventory system is in use, the flow of manufacturing costs through the company's accounting system closely parallels the physical flow of goods through the production process. Six accounts are typically used to account for manufacturing activities: (a) Materials Inventory, (b) Direct Labor, (c) Manufacturing Overhead, (d) Work in Process Inventory, (e) Finished Goods Inventory, and (f) Cost of Goods sold.

18. The *Materials Inventory* account is used to record purchases of direct materials and the use of these materials in the manufacturing process. *Direct materials* are those raw materials and components that constitute an integral part of finished products. Such materials can be traced directly to the finished products – such as windshields, transmissions, and tires in an automotive plant. Raw materials which cannot be conveniently traced to finished products are termed *indirect*

materials and are classified as part of ***manufacturing overhead***. Examples of indirect materials include lubricating oil and glue.

19. Direct material purchases are debited directly to the ***Materials Inventory*** account. As these materials are used in production, their costs are transferred from the Materials Inventory account into the ***Work in Process Inventory*** account (debit work in Process Inventory, credit Materials Inventory). The balance remaining at year-end in the Materials Inventory account represents the cost of raw materials and components on hand and available for future use.

20. The ***Direct Labor*** account is used to record the cost of payrolls to workers whose efforts can be traced directly to the goods being manufactured. Examples include machine operators, assemblers, and painters. Many employees in a manufacturing facility, such as supervisors and security guards, do ***not*** participate directly in the manufacturing process. The costs associated with these employees are termed ***indirect*** labor and are considered part of ***manufacturing overhead***.

21. At each payroll date, the Direct Labor account is debited for the total amount of the direct labor payroll. As work is performed on the goods being manufactured, the related labor costs are transferred from the Direct Labor account into the Work in Process Inventory account (debit Work in Process Inventory, credit Direct Labor).

22. The ***Manufacturing Overhead*** account is used to record all costs classified as "overhead," and to assign being manufactured. Manufacturing overhead is a broad category of manufacturing costs that represents all manufacturing costs other than direct materials and direct labor.

23. Selling expenses and general and administrative expenses do ***not*** relate to the manufacturing process and are ***not*** included in manufacturing overhead. All costs of storing, marketing, or delivering finished goods are viewed as selling expenses. Costs incurred to operate a company's accounting, legal, and personnel departments are considered general and administrative expenses.

24. The ***Manufacturing Overhead*** account is originally debited to record any cost classified as "overhead," such as purchases of indirect materials, indirect labor costs, and depreciation on machinery. As these items are "consumed" by the production process, the related costs are transferred from the Manufacturing Overhead account into the Work in Process Inventory account (debit Work in Process Inventory, credit Manufacturing Overhead). In the course of the year, all overhead costs incurred should be allocated to units manufactured, leaving a zero balance in the Manufacturing Overhead account.

25. The ***Work in Process Inventory***, account is used to (a) accumulate the manufacturing costs relating to all units worked during the period, and (b) to allocate these costs among those units completed during the period and those that are only partially completed at year-end. As materials are placed into production and manufacturing activities take place, the related costs are ***debited*** to the Work in Process Inventory account. As specific units are completed, the costs associated with manufacturing these units are transferred to the Finished Goods Inventory (debit Finished Goods Inventory, credit Work in Process Inventory). The ending balance in the Work in Process Inventory account represents the manufacturing costs associated with those units still "in process" at year-end.

26. As finished goods are sold, their costs are transferred from the Finished Goods Inventory account into the Cost of Goods Sold account (debit Cost of Goods Sold, credit Finished Goods Inventory).

27. Transferring the cost of specific units from one account to another requires knowledge of the ***per-unit cost*** – that is, the total direct material, direct labor, and manufacturing overhead costs applicable to specific units. A knowledge of per-unit manufacturing costs is useful to managers in making pricing decisions, evaluating production efficiency, and planning future operations.

28. Most manufacturing companies prepare a schedule of the cost of finished goods manufactured to provide managers with an overview of manufacturing costs for the period. The bottom line of the schedule shows the *cost of finished goods manufactured* during the current period.

29. The format and content of a schedule of the cost of finished goods manufactured is illustrated below:

Work in process, beginning of period	$XXX

Add manufacturing costs:

Direct materials used	$XXX	
Direct labor	XXX	
Manufacturing overhead	XXX	
Total manufacturing costs		XXX

Total cost of all goods in process during the period	$XXX
Less: Work in process end of period	(XXX)
Cost of finished goods manufactured	$XXX

30. If a company manufactures only a single product, the *per-unit cost* can be determined by simply dividing the cost of finished goods manufactured by the number of units produced. If a company manufactures multiple product lines, a separate schedule of the cost of finished goods manufactured can be prepared for each line.

31. The manufacturing costs relating to units sold during the period appear in the *income statement* as the *cost of goods sold*, Manufacturing costs relating to raw materials partially completed products, and to finished goods on hand at year-end appear as *inventory* in the company's *balance sheet*.

TEST YOURSELF ON MANAGEMENT ACCOUNTING

True or False

For each of the following statements, circle the T or the F to indicate whether the statement is true or false.

T F   1.   Managers are rarely assigned decision-making authority over a firm's assets.

T F   2.   The linked set of activities and resources necessary to create and deliver products or services to customers is referred to as benchmarking activities.

T F   3.   Accounting systems often provide parallel monitoring capabilities to serve the information needs of internal parties (managers) and external parties (investors and creditors).

T F   4.   There are currently no professional certifications available for those who wish to pursue careers in management accounting.

T F   5.   Management accounting reports should be presented in accordance with generally accepted accounting principles.

T F   6.   An inventory of finished goods is an asset, but inventories of raw materials and work in process are not considered assets until production is completed.

T F   7.   Manufacturing costs are regarded as period costs and are reported in the income statement for the current period.

T F   8.   Product costs are the costs of purchasing or manufacturing inventory and represent assets until the goods are sold.

T F   9.   Selling, general, and administrative expenses are all examples of product costs.

T F   10. All costs and expenses incurred by a manufacturing company are considered product costs rather than period costs.

T F   11. If the levels of finished goods and work in process inventories are increasing, the amount of product cost deducted from revenue during the period will be less than the amount of product costs incurred.

T F   12. A manufacturing company usually has three separate inventories: materials, manufacturing supplies, and finished goods.

T F   13. Materials inventory refers to the direct materials on hand and available for use in the manufacturing process.

T F   14. Manufacturing companies do not use perpetual inventory systems because such systems do not parallel the physical flow of goods through the production process.

T F   15. Direct materials are those raw materials that become an integral part of finished products such as nails, glue and lubricating oil.

T F   16. Manufacturing overhead includes all manufacturing costs except direct labor and direct materials.

T F   17. The wages paid to supervisors are an example of direct labor.

T F   18. Product costs are all deducted from revenue in the period in which they are incurred.

T F   19. Product costs associated with work in process and unsold inventories of finished goods appear in the balance sheet as current assets until the goods are sold.

T F   20. Some costs, such as property taxes, should be allocated between manufacturing overhead and operating expenses.

T F   21. The Work in Process Inventory account reports only the cost of partially completed products at year-end.

T F   22. Costs incurred to store and to ship finished products are considered product costs.

T F   23. The schedule of the cost of finished goods manufactured is a required financial statement for manufacturing companies.

Completion Statements

Fill in the necessary word to complete the following statements:

1. A _____ _____ is the linked set of activities and resources necessary to create and deliver products or services to customers.

2. More and more organizations are sharing information by participating in and undertaking _____ _____.

3. Management accounting information is used primarily by _____ to assist them in making business decisions.

4. The major classifications of manufacturing costs are _____ _____, _____ _____, and _____ _____.

5. Manufacturing costs are the costs of creating inventory and are termed _____ _____. Costs that are charged directly to expense accounts are termed _____ _____. Product costs are transferred from the balance sheet to the _____ _____ when the goods are sold.

6. Manufacturing companies have three inventory categories: (a) _____ _____, (b) _____ ____ _____ _____, and (c) _____ _____ _____.

7. The term _____ _____ refers to integral materials and component parts that can be directly traced to finished products. Materials on hand and available for use at the end of the period are represented by the balance in the _____ _____ account.

8. A machine operator's salary would be accounted for in the _____ _____ account, while the salary of a production supervisor would be accounted for in the _____ _____ account.

9. As specific units are completed, the cost of manufacturing them is transferred by _____ the Finished Goods Inventory account and _____ the Work in Process Inventory account.

10. In a merchandising company, the cost of goods sold is based upon the cost of _____ merchandise for resale. In a manufacturing company, it is based on the costs of _____ these products.

11. Shown below is information for a manufacturing company: (all figures are stated in dollars):

Cost of direct materials ....$ 80,000
Direct labor.. 200,000
Total manufacturing costs incurred...................................... 400,000
Total cost of work in process during the year 450,000
Work in process inventory, year-end 20,000
Decrease in finished goods inventory during the year 7,500

From the information given above, provide the following information: (a) Work in process inventory at the beginning of the year: $_____; (b) manufacturing overhead costs for the year: $_____; (c) the cost of finished goods manufactured for the year: $_____; and (d) the cost of goods sold for the year: $_____.

Multiple Choice

Choose the best answer for each of the following questions and enter the identifying letter in the space provided.

___ 1. Which of the following is *not* one of the three principles that govern the design of a management accounting system?

    a. Deciding who has decision-making authority over business assets.

    b. Producing information to support decision making processes.

    c. Providing a means of monitoring, evaluating, and rewarding performance.

    d. Determining a market value of a corporation's stock.

___ 2. The two exams sponsored by the Institute of Certified Management Accounts are the:

    a. CMA exam and the CPA exam.

    b. CFM exam and the CPA exam.

    c. CPA exam and the ICMA exam.

    d. CMA exam and the CFM exam.

___ 3. Users of Management accounting reports would include:

    a. A prospective investor deciding whether to purchase a company's bonds.

    b. A prospective investor deciding whether to purchase a company's stock.

    c. A sales manager determining a market price for a company's products.

    d. A shareholder determining whether a company has been profitable.

___ 4. Manufacturing costs would *not* include:

    a. Indirect materials used.

    b. Income tax expense.

    c. Indirect labor costs.

    d. Depreciation of factory equipment.

5. Each of the following statements is true with respect to product costs *except*:
   a. Product costs represent inventoriable costs.

   b. Product costs are deducted from revenue when the manufacturing process is completed.

   c. Product costs are not necessarily regarded as expenses of the current period.

   d. Direct labor is an example of a product cost.

6. Which of the following is *not* likely to be treated as a product cost?
   a. Depreciation of the factory equipment.

   b. A portion of the cost of running the quality control department.

   c. Salaries paid to factory workers.

   d. Interest paid on bonds payable.

7. The Materials Inventory account is *credited* when:
   a. Direct materials are purchased.

   b. Indirect materials are purchased.

   c. Direct materials are placed into production.

   d. Indirect materials are placed into production.

8. The Direct Labor account is *debited*:
   a. When related labor costs are transferred into the Work in Process Inventory account.

   b. At the end of each payroll period to record direct labor costs incurred during the period.

   c. As manufactured goods are completed.

   d. When a new factory employee begins work.

9. Turner Corporation produces kitchen cabinets. Which of the following materials would Turner account for in its Materials Inventory account?
   a. Sand paper for the electric sanders.

   b. Nails.

   c. Decorative knobs for the drawers.

   d. Glue for the joints.

10. The cost of finished goods manufactured is computed as follows:
   a. Ending work in process inventory plus direct materials used, direct labor, and manufacturing overhead; minus beginning work in process inventory.

   b. Beginning work in process inventory plus direct materials purchased, direct labor, and manufacturing overhead; minus ending work in process inventory.

   c. Beginning work in process inventory plus direct materials used, direct labor, and manufacturing overhead; minus ending work in process inventory.

   d. Beginning finished goods inventory plus direct materials used, direct labor, and manufacturing overhead; minus ending finished goods inventory.

Exercises

1. Listed below are six technical accounting terms emphasized in this chapter.

   Direct materials   *Manufacturing overhead*
   Product costs   *Materials inventory*
   Period costs   *Work in process inventory*

   Each of the following statements may (or may not) describe one of these technical terms. In the space provided below each statement, indicate the accounting term described, or answer "None" if the statement does not correctly describe any of the terms.

   a. Raw materials that become an integral part of manufactured goods and can be traced directly to finished goods.

   _____

   b. The completed units that have emerged from the manufacturing process and are on hand and available for sale.

   _____

   c. A category including all manufacturing costs other than the costs of direct materials used and direct labor.

   _____

   d. The costs of purchasing or manufacturing inventory that represent an asset until the related inventory is sold.

   _____

   e. Units in production that are not yet completed nor available for sale.

   _____

2. Indicate into which of the three manufacturing cost elements each item would be classified. Use the following symbols: **DM** for direct materials, **MO** for manufacturing overhead, **DL** for direct labor, and **X** for items which are not manufacturing costs.

   _____ a. Wages of a plant supervisor
   _____ b. Wages of a drill-press operator
   _____ c. Electricity used in factory operations
   _____ d. Property taxes on factory buildings
   _____ e. Property taxes o administrative buildings
   _____ f. Wages of a sales manager
   _____ g. Depreciation on factory machinery
   _____ h. Wood used by a furniture manufacturer
   _____ i. Glue used by a furniture manufacturer
   _____ j. Glass used by a window manufacturer

3. The information below was taken from the accounting records of Kiwi Cotton Products for the month:

Work in process inventory, beginning of the month	$ 22,000
Cost of direct materials used	210,000
Direct labor cost applied to production	80,000
Cost of finished goods manufactured.................................	380,000
Cost of manufacturing overhead applied to Production	120,000

Compute the amount of work in process inventory on hand at the end of the month.

4. The accounting records of Bright Electronics Inc., include the following information for the year:

	Dec 31	Jan. 1
Inventory of materials	$ 15,000	$ 18,000
Inventory of work in process...	11,000	9,000
Inventory of finished goods...	84,000	78,000
Direct materials used...	198,000	
Direct labor applied to production.....................................	132,000	
Manufacturing overhead applied to production	165,000	
Selling expenses	150,000	
General and administrative expenses	125,000	

a. Prepare a schedule of the cost of finished goods manufactured.

Schedule

Work in process, Jan.1		$ 9,000

b. Assume that the company manufactures a single product and that 20,000 units were completed during the year. What is the average cost per unit of manufacturing this product?

SOLUTIONS TO CHAPTER 16 SELF-TEST

True or False

1. **F** To achieve organizational goals, managers are often assigned decision-making authority for some of the firm's assets. For example, plant managers typically are responsible for decisions about equipment in the plant, physical plant layout, and sources of supplies and materials.

2. **F** The linked set of activities and resources necessary to create and deliver products or services to customers is referred to as the value chain.

3. **T** Accounting systems are designed to serve the information needs both internal and external parties. Accounting systems must be designed to fulfill the needs of a diverse audience, simultaneously.

4. **F** Professional certifications are available for those who plan to make a career in management accounting. The Institute of Management Accountants sponsors two certification exams, the Certified Management Accountant (CMA) exam, and the Certified in Financial Management (CFM) exam. To become either a CMA or a CFM, an individual must meet educational and experience requirements and pass a rigorous examination.

5. **F** Management accounting reports contain information relevant to the needs of management. As these reports are not distributed to outsiders, they need not be presented in accordance with generally accepted accounting principles or any other standard.

6. **F** Inventories of finished goods, work in process, and materials all represent assets and will appear in the balance sheet.

7. **F** Manufacturing costs are the costs of producing inventory, which is an asset. Period costs are regarded as expenses of the current period and are expensed when incurred.

8. **T** Product costs are often termed *inventoriable costs* and represent an asset until goods are sold.

9. **F** Selling, general, and administrative expenses are all examples of period costs.

10. **F** Costs which are directly associated with the manufacturing process are termed *product costs*; those not directly associated are *period costs*.

11. **T** An increase in inventory levels occurs when the quantity of goods manufactured exceeds the quantity sold.

12. **F** A manufacturing company's inventory accounts include Materials, Work in Process, and Finished Goods.

13. **T** Materials Inventory would include all direct materials purchased but not yet put into manufacturing process.

14. **F** Manufacturing companies may use either a perpetual or a periodic inventory system.

15. **F** Nails, glue and lubricating oil are all examples of *indirect* materials and would be accounted for as part of *manufacturing overhead*.

16. **T** To the extent that costs such as property taxes relate to manufacturing operations they are product costs and should be included in manufacturing overhead. To the extent that such costs do not relate to manufacturing operations, they are period costs and should be included in the operating expenses for the period.

17. **F** The wages paid to factory supervisors are an example of *indirect labor*.

18. **F** Product costs are deducted from revenue in the period in which the related goods are sold.

19. **T** Product costs relating to unsold goods appear in the balance sheet as inventory.

20. **T** Costs which are applicable to both manufacturing operations and other functions should be allocated among the Manufacturing Overhead account (a product cost) and the appropriate operating expense accounts (period costs).

21. **T** Costs related to units completed are transferred from the Work in Process Inventory account to the Finished Goods Inventory account. Costs related to partially completed units remain in the Work in Process account.

22. **F** Costs incurred after all manufacturing activities have been completed are viewed as period costs.

23. **F** A schedule of the cost finished goods manufactured is *not* a required financial statement.

Completion Statements

1. Value chain. 2. Benchmarking studies. 3. Managers. 4. Direct materials, direct labor, manufacturing overhead. 5. Product costs, period costs, income statement. 6. (a) Materials inventory, (b) work in process inventory, (c) finished goods inventory. 7. Direct materials, Materials inventory. 8. Direct labor, Manufacturing overhead. 9. Debiting, crediting. 10. Purchasing (or buying), manufacturing (or making). 11. (a) $50,000 ($450,000 - $400,000). (b) $120,000 ($400,000 - $80,000 - $200,000). (c) $430,000 ($450,000 -$20,000), (d) $437,500 ($430,000 + $7,500).

Multiple Choice

1. Answer **d**—Stock values are determined independent of management accounting systems. The primary principles governing the design of management accounting systems include the assignment of decision-making authority, assistance in making managerial decisions, monitoring the effectiveness of managerial decisions, and rewarding effective performance.

2. Answer **d**—The Certified Management Accountant (CMA) exam and the Certified in Financial Management (CFM) exam are both sponsored by the Institute of Certified Management Accountants (ICMA). The Certified Public Accountant (CPA) exam is written and administered by the American Institute of Certified Public Accountants (AICPA).

3. Answer **c**—Management accounting information is designed to assist managers in decision making. Managerial reports are not distributed to persons outside of the firm. Bond holders, prospective investors, and shareholders would all base their decisions primarily on financial statements.

4. Answer **b**—income tax expense is termed a period cost because income taxes are not associated with the manufacture of inventory. As such, they are charged directly to an expense account as they are incurred and do not enter into the computation of inventory.

5. Answer **b**—product costs represent inventory. As such, they are deducted from revenue when related goods are *sold*.

6. Answer **d**—since interest paid on bonds is not directly associated with the manufacturing process, it is treated as a period cost and expensed when incurred.

7. Answer **c**—when direct materials are placed into production, their cost is transferred from the Materials Inventory account into the Work in Process Inventory account by a debit to Work in Process Inventory and a credit to Materials Inventory.

8. Answer **b**—the Direct Labor account is used to record the cost of payroll to direct labor workers and to assign these costs to the goods being manufactured. It is debited at each payroll date and is credited when related labor costs are transferred into the Work in Process Inventory account.

9. Answer **c**—decorative knobs for the drawers are an example of a direct material and is thus accounted for in the Material Inventory account. Answers **a**, **b**, and **d** are all materials which

cannot be traced conveniently too finished goods. Thus, they are considered ***indirect materials*** and are classified as part of manufacturing overhead.

10.   Answer **c**—the schedule of finished goods manufactured summarizes the flow of manufacturing summarizes the flow of manufacturing costs into and out of the Work in Process Inventory account.

Solutions to Exercises

1.

  a. Direct materials

  b. None (This statement refers to Finished Goods Inventory.)

  c. Manufacturing overhead

  d. Product costs

  e. Work in process inventory

2.

  a. MO

  b. DL

  c. MO

  d. MO

  e. X

  f. X

  g. MO

  h. DM

  i. MO

  j. DM

3.

Work in process inventory, beginning of the month		$ 22,000
Add: Direct materials	$210,000	
Direct labor	80,000	
Manufacturing overhead	120,000	
Total manufacturing costs		410,000
Total cost of all goods in process during the month		$432,000
Less: Cost of finished goods manufactured		($380,000)
Work in process inventory, end of the month		$ 52,000

4.

a.

Work in process inventory, beginning of the year		$ 9,000
Add: Direct materials used	$198,000	
Direct labor	132,000	
Manufacturing overhead	165,000	
Total manufacturing costs		495,000
Total cost of all goods in process during the year		$504,000
Less: Work in process inventory, end of the year		(11,000)
Cost of finished goods manufactured		$493,000

b.

$24.65 average cost per unit (493,000 ÷ 20,000 units)

JOB ORDER COST SYSTEMS AND OVERHEAD ALLOCATIONS

Highlights of the Chapter

1. An organization's accounting system must provide a good "map" that links the costs and processes used to the goods and/or services created. Processes used to create goods and services vary widely. Tracking and measuring resources consumed by different types of manufacturing processes requires that a cost accounting system be in place.

2. *Cost accounting systems* are the methods and techniques used by enterprises to track resources consumed in creating and delivering products and/or services to customers. In manufacturing companies, cost accounting systems help to attain two important management objectives: (1) to determine unit manufacturing costs, and (2) to provide managers with useful information for planning and control.

3. Cost accounting systems are typically designed to accommodate the specific needs of individual companies. In Chapter 17, we discuss two approaches for measuring and tracking resource consumption: (1) job order costing, and (2) activity-based costing.

4. *Job order costing* is often used by companies that tailor their goods or services to the specific needs of individual customers. In job order costing, the costs of direct materials, direct labor, and manufacturing overhead and accumulated separately for each job. A "job" represents the goods manufactured or the services provided to fill a particular order or to produce a "batch" of a particular product. If a job contains multiple units of product, unit costs are determined by dividing the total cost charged to the job by the number of units produced.

5. *Activity-based costing (ABC)* tracks costs to the activities that consume resources. Manufacturing overhead costs are the primary focus of ABC. Unlike direct materials and direct labor, overhead costs cannot be traced directly to individual products or services. ABC helps managers to better understand the nature of these indirect costs.

6. *Job costs sheets* provide information necessary to track the consumption of resources in a job order cost system. A separate job cost sheet is prepared for each job. Many job costing software programs are available on the market today. Thus, job costs "sheets" pertaining to individual jobs or projects are often electronic records generated by, and stored on, computers.

7. In a perpetual inventory system, the Materials Inventory account (a "controlling" account) is debited for the cost of direct materials purchased during the period. Individual accounts in the materials subsidiary ledger are also debited at this time. Production departments must present a materials requisition form in order to obtain materials from the materials warehouse. The requisition shows the quantity of material needed and the job for which it will be used. The accounting department uses a copy of each requisition form to enter the cost of requisitioned materials on the appropriate job cost sheets, and to make proper credits to the materials subsidiary ledger. The month-end summary entry to account for materials placed into production include a debit to Work in Process Inventory and a credit to the Materials Inventory controlling account.

8. Debits to the Direct Labor account are made when direct laborers are paid (with corresponding credits made to Wages Payable or Cash). The Direct Labor account is credited for the cost of work performed (with a corresponding debit made to Work in Process Inventory). Time cards show the hours spent by each employee on each job and enable the accounting department to charge the appropriate direct labor cost to each job cost sheet. At the end of each accounting period, a summary entry is made by debiting the Work in Process Inventory account and crediting

the Direct Labor account for all direct labor charged to jobs during the period. A credit balance remaining in the Direct Labor account after the summary entry is made represents a liability for accrued wages payable.

9. The manufacturing Overhead account is debited for the actual amount of overhead costs incurred during the period. A predetermined *overhead application rate* is then used to assign an appropriate amount of this cost to specific jobs. The entry to apply costs to job sheets usually is made as specific jobs are completed. However, overhead costs are also applied to jobs that are still in process at the end of each accounting period. The summary entry made at the end of each accounting period (representing total manufacturing overhead costs charged to individual job costs sheets) includes a debit to the Work in Process Inventory account and a credit to the Manufacturing Overhead account.

10. Predetermined overhead application rates are based on estimates. Thus, applied overhead will rarely equal actual amounts incurred. A debit balance remaining in the Manufacturing Overhead account is called *underapplied* overhead, whereas a credit balance is termed *overapplied* overhead. Under-or overapplied amounts are usually allowed to accumulate throughout the year as they tend to "balance out" from month to month. At year-end any remaining balance may be closed directly to the Cost of Goods sold account if the amount is not considered "material." A material amount, however, should be apportioned among the Work in Process Inventory, Finished Goods Inventory, and Cost of Goods Sold accounts.

11. As each job is completed, its job cost sheet is removed from the work in process subsidiary ledger. The total cost shown on the sheet is transferred from the Work in Process Inventory account by debiting Finished Goods Inventory and crediting Work in Process Inventory.

12. When sales occur, two entries are necessary in a perpetual inventory system: (a) a debit to Cash (or Accounts Receivable) and a credit to Sales for the *sales price*, and (b) a debit to Cost of Goods Sold and a credit to Finished Goods Inventory for the *cost* of the goods sold (the direct materials, direct labor, and manufacturing overhead assigned to the goods).

13. Job order costing is appropriate when each unit of product or "batch" of production, is manufactured to different specifications. Many companies, however, produce a *continuous stream of identical units*. When identical products are produced in a continuous stream, there are no distinct "jobs." Therefore, companies engaging in mass production often use *process costing* rather than job order costing.

14. *Activity-based costing* is based on the premise that overhead costs are generated by a variety of different activities. Such activities may relate to the moving and storage of raw materials, the set-up of equipment, the disposal of wastes, utility costs, etc.

15. In an activity-based costing system, different activity bases and overhead application rates are used to apply different types of overhead costs to production, which results in a better measure of a product's "true" cost.

16. In an activity-based costing system, overhead costs are first assigned to various *activity cost pools* representing specific activities which generate overhead costs (materials handling pool, equipment set-up pool, building maintenance pool, etc.). Separate overhead application rates are often used to assign costs to each pool. For instance, a company may assign the cost of electricity to a heating cost pool or a machinery cost pool using kilowatt-hour requirements as an activity base.

17. Having assigned manufacturing overhead to activity cost pools, each pool is then allocated to products based on the most appropriate cost drivers. For example, a heating cost pool may be assigned to products based on the square feet of manufacturing space occupied by each line. Likewise, a machinery cost pool might be allocated to products based on the number of machine-hours required to manufacture batches of each line.

18.   In short, an activity-based costing system recognizes that product lines have speical overhead considerations and requirements. The use of a single activity base (direct labor hours, machine-hours, etc.) ignores these factors and can result in cost allocation distortions.

19.   The potential benefits of activity-based costing are numerous: (a) better measures of a product's "true" per-unit manufacturing costs, (b) realistic and competitive pricing strategies, (c) the identification of production inefficiency, and (d) enhanced understanding of and control over product costs without sacrificing quality.

TEST YOURSELF ON ACCOUNTING SYSTEMS FOR MEASURING COSTS

True or False

For each of the following statements, circle the T or the F to indicate whether the statement is true or false.

T   F   1.   The concepts of cost accounting are applicable to banks, hospitals, and government agencies, as well as to manufacturing businesses.

T   F   2.   A job order cost system is one that traces manufacturing costs to specific processes of production.

T   F   3.   Effective control of costs in a manufacturing facility is possible only by using a well-designed cost accounting system.

T   F   4.   If a company manufacturers only one product, and recorded cost figures contain no arithmetical errors, the precise cost of manufacturing a unit of production in a given period can be computed.

T   F   5.   In a job order cost system, the cost of direct materials used in production is debited to the Materials Inventory account as materials are requisitioned.

T   F   6.   In a job order cost system, overhead costs may be applied only to jobs that are completed.

T   F   7.   The Materials Inventory account is supported by a subsidiary ledger consisting of job cost sheets.

T   F   8.   The allocation of factory overhead to units of output is accomplished by relating factory overhead to some other cost factor, such as direct labor hours, which can be identified with units produced.

T   F   9.   The use of predetermined overhead rates in a job cost system eliminates the need for recording actual overhead costs incurred during the period.

T   F   10.   The use of predetermined overhead rates in a job cost system makes it possible to estimate a total cost figure for given jobs as soon as they are completed.

T   F   11.   A debit balance in the Manufacturing Overhead account at the end of the period indicates that overhead has been underapplied to jobs.

T F 12. If the year-end balance in the Manufacturing Overhead account is material in dollar amount, it is applied entirely to the Cost of Goods sold account.

T F 13. When job cost systems are used in a perpetual inventory environment, the cost of goods sold is recorded as goods are transferred to finished goods.

T F 14. The current manufacturing environment is characterized by efforts to improve production efficiency, product quality, and per-unit manufacturing cost information.

T F 15. Companies that manufacture hundreds of products are less likely to require an activity-based costing system than companies that manufacture a single product line.

T F 16. In an activity-based costing system, manufacturing overhead costs are assigned to products prior to being allocated to activity cost pools.

T F 17. Direct labor hours would most likely be an inappropriate cost driver for allocating an electricity cost pool to product lines.

T F 18. The use of a single activity base (or cost driver) to assign manufacturing overhead to products can distort unit cost computations, but will not result in unrealistic pricing decisions.

T F 19. Activity-based costing systems can help managers identify inefficient aspects of the production process.

T F 20. Activity-based costing allocates manufacturing overhead to products in proportion to the relative sales volume of each product line.

Completion Statements

Fill in the necessary word to complete the following statements:

1. Two important managerial objectives served by a cost accounting system are: (a) to determine _____-_____ costs, and, (b) to provide information useful in _____ and _____ business operations.

2. In a job cost system, the Materials Inventory account is debited for the total amount of materials _____ during the period and credited for the total amount of materials _____ during the period.

3. Assume that a particular job cost system applies manufacturing overhead to production at a rate of 150% of direct labor costs. If a certain job required 300 hours of direct labor at an average rate of $20 per hour, its job cost sheet would be charged with $_____ of manufacturing overhead.

4. In a job cost system, the _____ _____ _____ constitute the subsidiary ledger for the Work in Process Inventory account.

5. If the Manufacturing Overhead account has a debit balance at the end of the year, overhead has been _____, and the _____ _____ _____ _____ reported on the company's income statement will be understated unless an appropriate adjustment is made.

6. Activity-based costing is a relatively new approach to the problem of allocating _____ _____ to product lines.

7. The use of machine-hours as an activity base may not be an appropriate cost driver for products that are highly (labor/capital) _____ intensive.

8. In an activity-based costing system, costs are first assigned to _____ _____ _____ before allocated to specific product lines.

9. One major goal of activity-based costing is to determine more accurate _____- _____ manufacturing overhead costs.

10. To be appropriate, an activity base must be a significant _____ _____ of manufacturing overhead costs.

Multiple Choice

Choose the best answer for each of the following questions and enter the identifying letter in the space provided.

___ 1. A job order cost system is often used when:
    a. A single product is manufactured.

    b. Products are manufactured to the specifications of individual customers.

    c. Manufacturing overhead costs are substantially less than direct labor costs.

    d. The cost of direct materials is substantially greater than overhead costs.

___ 2. Which of the following is *not* true regarding job cost sheets?
    a. A separate job cost sheet is prepared for each job.

    b. A job cost sheet is used to accumulate all manufacturing costs charged to a particular production department during the period.

    c. Costs are accumulated on a job cost sheet include direct materials, direct labor, and applied manufacturing overhead.

    d. A job cost sheet is used to compute unit costs of production.

___ 3. In a job order cost system, the subsidiary ledger for the Work in Process Inventory controlling account consists of:
    a. Job cost sheets.

    b. Materials requisitions.

    c. Employee time cards.

    d. Work in process inventory records for various processing departments.

_ 4. The journal entry to record the transfer of units to the Finished Goods Inventory typically includes:

    a. A debit to Cost of Goods sold and a credit to Work in Process Inventory.

    b. A debit to Work in Process Inventory and a credit to Finished Goods Inventory.

    c. A debit to Finished Goods Inventory and a credit to Work in Process Inventory.

    d. None of these.

_ 5. Over-or underapplied overhead:

    a. Occurs only when a job order cost system is in use.

    b. Occurs only when a process cost system is in use.

    c. Does not occur when a predetermined overhead application rate is used to apply overhead to work in process.

    d. Is closed to the Cost of Goods sold account at year-end if the amount is not considered material.

_ 6. Which of the following would be the *least* appropriate cost driver in assigning production set-up costs to product lines?

    a. Number of set-ups required.

    b. Number of production runs per product line.

    c. Total set-up hours required per product line.

    d. Direct labor dollars per product line.

_ 7. A specific aspect of the production process to which manufacturing overhead costs can be traced is called:

    a. A product line.

    b. An activity cost pool.

    c. A profit center.

    d. A production run.

_ 8. The use of a single activity base to allocate manufacturing overhead to products may:

    a. Distort per-unit costs.

    b. Improve product quality.

    c. Increase efficiency.

    d. Enhance management's understanding of cost behavior.

_ 9. To be reliable, an activity base must be a significant:

    a. Source of revenue.

    b. Area of inefficiency.

    c. Measure of company growth.

    d. Cost driver.

10. Which of the following is *not* considered a benefit of activity-based costing systems?

    a.   Improved quality.

    b.   More accurate measurement of per-unit manufacturing costs.

    c.   Ease of design and implementation.

    d.   Competitive pricing strategies.

Exercises

1. Listed below are six technical accounting terms emphasized in this chapter.

Activity-based costing	*Cost driver*
Job order costing	*Cost accounting systems*
Overhead application rate	*Underapplied overhead*

Each of the following statements may (or may not) describe one of these technical terms. In the space provided below each statement, indicate the accounting term described, or answer "None" if the statement does not correctly describe any of the terms.

a. A casual factor in the incurrence of overhead costs.

_____

b. A cost accounting method that tracks indirect costs to activities that consume resources.

_____

c. A record used to summarize the manufacturing costs associated with a particular job or batch of production.

_____

d. Methods and techniques used to track the cost of resources consumed in creating products and delivering services to customers.

_____

e. A predetermined figure used to assign manufacturing overhead costs to production.

_____

f. A credit balance remaining in the Manufacturing Overhead account at the end of the year.

_____

2. The Magic Forest Company builds custom vacation cabins and uses a job order cost system. Overhead is applied to individual jobs at a rate of 60% of the direct labor costs incurred per job.

A cabin built for Avery Jones required $40,000 of materials and $15,000 of direct labor. The cabin was started and completed in April of the current year.

At the end of the current year, the company's total direct labor costs incurred were $320,000, and actual overhead amounted to $208,000.

a. The cost of the Jones cabin as shown on its job cost sheet on the date of completion was:

Direct material...$
Direct labor...
Overhead ...._____
    Total cost...$____

b. Was overhead for the entire year on all jobs overapplied or underapplied? Explain.

c. What should the company do to account for the difference between actual overhead and applied overhead at the end of the year?

3. Listed below are eight activity cost pools used by American Tool Corporation (ATC).

Machinery set-up costs   *Employee training costs*
Design costs   *Heating costs*
Machinery power costs   *Materials warehouse costs*
Purchasing department costs   *Quality inspection costs*

The following activity bases are used by ATC to allocate these activity cost pools to its products. For each activity base, indicate the activity cost pool for which it is the most appropriate cost driver.

a. Square feet of space required to store the component parts of each product line.
   _____

b. Number of machine-hours required to product a batch of each product line.
   _____

c. Number of new hires related to each product line.
   _____

d. Number of production runs for each product line.
   _____

33

e.   Number of engineering of change orders generated by each product line.

_____

f.   Square feet of production space occupied by each product line.

_____

g.   Number of raw materials, purchase orders generated for each product line.

_____

h.   Defective units per thousand units manufactured of each product line.

_____

4.   Glamour, Inc. has two product lines: mass produced jewelry and custom-made jewelry. The company assigns $15,000 of its monthly overhead to two cost pools: (1) heating costs, and (2) supervisory costs. The heating pool receives approximately $1,000, whereas the supervisory cost pool receives $14,000. Heating costs are allocated to products based on the square-feet of production space occupied by each line. Supervisory costs pool are allocated to products based on the number of supervisors assigned to each line. The following monthly figures have been provided:

	Mass-Produced	Custom-Made
Direct labor and materials costs	$20,700	$40,300
Units produced and sold	5,000	500
Square feet of production space	1,600	400
Number of supervisors	1	3

Allocate the manufacturing overhead from the activity cost pools to each product line and compute the per-unit cost of each.

Solutions to Chapter 17 Self-Test

True or False

1.   **T** Although cost accounting systems are most widely used in manufacturing companies, the same concepts are used in many service industries to plan and control business activities.

2.   **F** A job order cost system accumulates costs separately for each job or batch of products.

3.   **T** Controlling costs involves keeping costs within acceptable limits. Managers must have timely information about current unit costs to evaluate cost control efforts. Such information is not possible without a well-designed cost accounting system.

4.   **F** Even in the situation described, the cost computed will be partially based upon estimates (such as depreciation expense on manufacturing equipment) and average costs (such as wage rates that may fluctuate throughout the accounting period).

5.   **F** The cost of direct materials used in production is **credited** to the Materials Inventory controlling account as the materials are requisitioned.

6.   **F** Although the entry to apply overhead costs to job sheets is usually made when the job is completed, overhead costs should also be applied to jobs still in process at the end of each period.

7. **F** Job cost sheets comprise the subsidiary ledger for the Work in Process Inventory controlling account. The Materials Inventory subsidiary ledger consists of accounts for each type of material used in production.

8. **T** The factors (such as machine-hours or direct labor hours) directly related to units of output are called *cost drivers* and are used in computing overhead application rates.

9. **F** Actual overhead costs are recorded as incurred. The overhead application rate is used to allocate a portion of these costs to actual jobs.

10. **T** Although there may be under-or overapplied overhead remaining at the end of each month, these amounts tend to balance out over the year. Thus, the cost of a completed job need not be adjusted unless the year-end balance is considered material.

11. **T** A debit balance indicates that actual overhead costs incurred exceeded the amount applied to jobs using a predetermined overhead application rate.

12. **F** If the year-end balance in the Manufacturing Overhead account is material, it should be apportioned among the Work in Process Inventory, Finished Goods Inventory, and the Cost of Goods Sold.

13. **F** The cost of goods sold is recorded as goods are sold and transferred out of finished goods inventory.

14. **T** To compete globally, companies must increase efficiency, manufacture quality products, and have access to accurate cost information.

15. **F** Many different processes are required to produce hundreds of product lines. An activity-based costing system results in a more accurate measure of product cost by applying overhead on the basis of processing activities required by each product line.

16. **F** In an activity-based costing system, overhead costs are assigned to activity cost pools prior to being allocated to individual products.

17. **T** Machine-hours or kilowatt hours would be more appropriate for allocating costs to products.

18. **F** Product pricing is based on unit-cost computations. Thus, if unit costs are distorted, prices are likely to be distorted as well.

19. **T** A primary benefit of activity-based costing systems is that they help managers identify those production processes that are performed efficiently and those that are not.

20. **F** An activity-based costing system allocated manufacturing overhead to products on the basis of processing activities required by each product line.

Completion Statements

1. (a) Per-unit, (b) planning, controlling. 2. Purchased, requisitioned. 3. $9,000. 4. Job cost sheets.

5. Under-applied, cost of goods sold. 6. Manufacturing overhead. 7. Labor. 8. Activity cost pools.

9. Per-unit. 10. Cost driver.

Multiple Choice

1. Answer **b**—answer **a** would indicate use of a process cost system. The type of cost accounting system most appropriate for a business depends upon the nature of its manufacturing activities and the type of products it produces, not the relative amounts of various manufacturing costs.

2. Answer **b**—costs are accumulated by department in a process cost system. In a job cost system, job cost sheets are used to accumulate costs for specific jobs.

3. Answer **a**—each job in a process has a job cost sheet. Costs are recorded on individual job cost sheets as well as in the Work in Process Inventory controlling account.

4. Answer **c**—the amount used in the entry is determined from a job cost sheet in a job cost system, or from unit cost date in a process cost system.

5. Answer **d**—over-or underapplied overhead may occur in either type of cost accounting system. It is a direct result of using a predetermined overhead application rate to apply overhead costs to work in process.

6. Answer **d**—production set-up costs are not likely to vary in direct proportion to direct labor hours. As such, direct labor hours would not be a significant cost driver of set-up costs.

7. Answer **b**—activity cost pools represent processing activities to which manufacturing overhead costs can be traced.

8. Answer **a**—different products require different processing activities. As such, allocating overhead to products on the basis of a single activity may distort the measurement of product costs.

9. Answer **d**—to be reliable, an activity base must be significant cost driver of overhead costs. In other word, changes in the volume of the activity base must cause changes in overhead costs.

10. Answer **c**—activity-based costing systems have many benefits. However, they are also more difficult to design and implement than traditional costing systems.

Solutions to Exercise

1.
   a. Cost driver.
   b. Activity-based costing.
   c. None (This statement refers to a job cost sheet.)
   d. Cost accounting systems.
   e. Overhead application rate.
   f. None (This statement refers to overapplied overhead.)

2.
   a. The total cost of the Jones cabin as shown on its job cost sheet on the date of completion was:

Direct material	$40,000
Direct labor	15,000
Overhead	9,000
Total cost	$64,000

   b. Underapplied by $16,000. Actual overhead was $208,000. Overhead applied was $192,000, or 60% of direct labor ($320,000 x 60% = $192,000). Thus, $16,000 of overhead was not charged to production.

   c. The under applied overhead of $16,000 should be charged to the Cost of Goods Sold account (assuming it is considered immaterial).

3.
   a. Materials warehouse costs
   b. Machinery power costs
   c. Employee training costs

d. Machinery set-up costs

e. Design costs

f. Heating costs

g. Purchasing department costs

h. Quality inspection costs

4.   Percent of production space occupied by each product line:

Mass-product 1,600 ÷ 2,000 = 80%

Custom-made   400 ÷ 2,000 = 20%

Percent of supervisors assigned to each product line:

Mass produced: 1÷4 = 25%.

Custom-made: 3÷4 = 75%.

Overhead costs allocated to each product line:

	Mass-Produced	Custom Made
Heating costs:		
$1,000 x 80%......................................	800	
$1,000 x 20%......................................		200
Supervisory costs:		
$14,000 x 25%....................................	3,500	
$14,000 x 75%....................................		10,500
Labor and materials costs.......................	20,700	40,300
Total costs allocated	$25,000	$51,000
Unit produced.....................................	5,000	500
Per-unit cost......................................	$ 5	$ 102

Highlights of the Chapter

1. Managers choose among many different *cost accounting systems* for their companies. These systems provide information used for many types of business decisions.

2. *Process costing*, like job order costing, is a method of accumulating both direct and indirect production costs. Unlike job order costing, which traces costs to specific jobs or unique projects, process costing averages direct and indirect costs across mass produced identical units.

3. Many businesses have multiple operations associated with creating goods or services. Some of these operations may be best suited for job order costing systems, while other operations may be best suited for process costing cost systems. Thus, it is not uncommon to find companies that use both job order and process costing systems simultaneously.

4. Process costing is most often associated with the production of a continuous stream of identical units, such as bottles of soda, gallons of gasoline, or cases of aspirin. These mass produced products often flow through a variety of production processes. Process costing systems measure the cost associated with *each process*, and then allocates these costs to the units produced during the period.

5. Process costing serves two related purposes. First, it measures the cost of goods manufactured on both a total and per-unit basis. This information is used in valuing inventory and in determining the cost of goods sold. Second, process costing provides management with information about the per-unit cost of performing each step in the production process. This information is useful in evaluating the *efficiency* of production departments.

6. Process costing uses separate Work in Process Inventory accounts to measure costs incurred in *each production process*. Costs flow through these accounts in sequence, just as units on an assembly line move from one production process to another.

7. Most companies that use process costing systems simply combine the cost of direct materials and manufacturing overhead. They do so because these two costs are incurred uniformly throughout production. The combined amount of direct material and manufacturing overhead is referred to as *conversion costs*.

8. Each Work in Process account is charged (debited) for the materials used, direct labor, and manufacturing overhead that relate to that specific process (or phase of production) . As units in production pass from one process to the next, process costing parallels the physical flow of these units by transferring their *cost* from one Work in Process account to the rest.

9. At the end of each accounting period, managers must account for any partially completed units which reside in the various production departments of the company. To recognize partially completed work in process units, companies use a technique referred to as *equivalent units*. Equivalent units provide a means of expressing partially completed units in terms of wholly completed units. For example, two units 50% complete are considered equivalent to one unit 100% complete. Companies use equivalent units to assign costs to inventories.

10. In each accounting period, equivalent whole units of materials, labor, and manufacturing overhead are "consumed" in order to: (1) complete units in process at the beginning of the period, (2) start and complete units during the period, and (3) start, but not complete, the units in process at the end of the period.

11. Assume that 100 partially completed units are process at the beginning of the period, and that each unit is 25% complete with respect to materials. The quantity of material needed to complete these units is equivalent to producing 75 completed units from "scratch" (100 units x 75% of the materials needed to *complete* them). Likewise, if 300 partially completed units remain in process at the end of the period, and each unit is 40% complete with respect to its materials, the quantity of material consumed during the period by these partially completed units is equivalent to producing 120 completed units from "scratch" (300 units x 40% of required materials consumed during the current period).

12. The units of production *started (from "scratch") and completed* during the period may be calculated in one of two ways: (1) units started during the period minus units in process at the end of the period, or (2) units transferred out of the department during the period minus units in process at the beginning of the period. For example, assume that a production department had 100 partially completed units in process at the beginning of the period, started 900 units during the current period, transferred 600 units to another department during the period, and had 400 units in process at the end of the period. Thus, *500 units* must have been started (from "scratch") and completed during the period, computed as follows: (1) 900 units started minus 400 units in process at the end of the period, or (2) 600 units transferred out during the period minus 100 units in process at the beginning of the period.

13. In computing units started and completed during the period, it is common to always assume a first-in, first-out (FIFO) cost flow. Thus, manufacturing costs are "tracked" in the following sequence during the period: (1) the first resources consumed during the period are associated with finishing those units in process at the beginning of the period, (2) the next resources consumed are associated with those units started (from "scratch") and completed during the period, and (3) any remaining resources consumed are associated with those units started during the current period that will not be completed until the following period (i.e., the units in ending work in process).

14. To determine the amount of cost to assign a specific production department—to finish its beginning work in process, to start and complete new units during the period, and to start, but not complete, those units in process at the end of the period—managers compute the *cost per equivalent unit* incurred during the period. This simple averaging technique divides the cost accumulated for each resource (materials, labor, and manufacturing overhead) by the associated number of equivalent units consumed during the period. These per unit costs are used to value the ending work in process of each department, the units in Finished Goods Inventory, and the Cost of Goods Sold reported in the income statement.

15. Unit cost data provided by a process costing system is used by managers to set sales prices, evaluate the manufacturing efficiency of individual departments, forecast future manufacturing costs, value inventories, and report the cost of goods sold.

16. In some automated manufacturing environments, units pass through production processes very quickly—often within several minutes or less. Thus, the number of units "in process" at any one point in time is insignificant in relation to the number of units processed during the month. For this reason, some companies ignore assigning costs to beginning and ending Work in Process and simply assign all production costs to those units *completed and transferred* during the period. Assigning all costs to units completed and transferred greatly simplifies process costing. In such cases, accountants need only make a series of month-end entries to transfer the total costs associated with each Work in Process account to the next (or from the final Work in Process account to Finished Goods Inventory).

17. Companies frequently present their results of operations for a period using *a production cost report*. The production cost report is a summary of all work completed during the period. The report shows the total cost of resources consumed as well as average unit costs in terms of

equivalent whole units. The summary report also identifies and reconciles the total costs to account for during the period. These costs are used to value inventory, determine the cost of goods sold, and to measure various aspects of production efficiency.

TEST YOURSELF ON ACCOUNTING SYSTEMS FOR MEASURING COSTS

True or False

For each of the following statements, circle the T or the F to indicate whether the statement is true or false.

T   F   1.   A process cost system is appropriate when production consists of uniform products such as paint, cement, or dairy products.

T   F   2.   Process cost systems typically use separate Work in Process Inventory accounts for each manufacturing (or processing) department.

T   F   3.   Companies rarely use job order cost systems and process costing systems simultaneously.

T   F   4.   In a process cost system, direct labor and manufacturing overhead costs are often lumped together as conversion costs.

T   F   5.   In a process cost system, costs are transferred directly from each department Work in Process account to the Finished Goods Inventory account.

T   F   6.   In some companies, the number of partially completed units in process at the end of each period is small relative to the total units completed and transferred to finished goods during the period.

T   F   7.   Unit costs in a process cost system are sometimes determined by dividing the total manufacturing costs for the period by the number of units completed and transferred to finished goods during the period.

T   F   8.   In a process cost system, units are often defined differently for each production (or processing) department.

T   F   9.   Job and process cost systems provide information exclusively for external reporting purposes.

T   F   10.   When job and process cost systems are used in a perpetual inventory environment, the cost of goods sold is recorded as goods are transferred to finished goods.

T   F   11.   As costs flow from one Work in Process account to the next in a process costing system, the Work in Process account *from* which costs are being transferred is debited, and the Work in Process account *to* which costs are being transferred is credited.

T   F   12.   As costs are transferred from the final Work in Process account in a process costing system, the Work in Process account is credited, and the Cost of Goods Sold account is debited.

T F   13. Equivalent units are used in a process costing system to enable managers to express product costs on the basis of whole units, as opposed to partially completed units.

T F   14. Some companies with highly automated manufacturing processes simply ignore beginning and ending Work in Process balances and assign all production costs to those units completed and transferred to Finished Goods during the month.

Completion Statements

Fill in the necessary word to complete the following statements:

1. _____ _____ _____ provide information used by managers to measure the cost of providing goods and services, to price products, and to evaluate efficiency.

2. _____ _____ is a method for accumulating costs over a continuous stream of identical units.

3. _____ _____ _____ systems trace costs to unique or specific jobs.

4. Direct labor and manufacturing overhead costs are often lumped together and called _____ _____.

5. To avoid having to express unit costs in terms of partially completed units, process costing systems measure costs in terms of _____ _____.

6. A detailed _____ _____ for a specified process in a process costing system details the flow of physical goods, equivalent units, total costs, and costs per equivalent unit.

Multiple Choice

Choose the best answer for each of the following questions and enter the identifying letter in the space provided.

___ 1. A process cost system is often used if a company:
   a. Engages in the mass production of homogeneous products.
   b. Is subject to substantial seasonal variation in the types of products manufactured.
   c. Produces a wide variety of products to varying specifications.
   d. Has only a single production process or department.

___ 2. The journal entry to record the transfer of units to the Finished Goods Inventory typically includes:
   a. A debit to Cost of Goods sold and a credit to Work in Process Inventory.
   b. A debit to Work in Process Inventory and a credit to Finished Goods Inventory.
   c. A debit to Finished Goods Inventory and a credit to Work in Process Inventory.
   d. None of these.

___ 3.   In a process cost system, the volume of partially completed units at the end of the period is sometimes:

    a.   Relatively large in comparison to the volume of units completed and transferred to finished goods during the period.

    b.   Relatively small in comparison to the volume of units completed and transferred to finished goods during the period.

    c.   Subtracted from the volume of units completed and transferred to finished goods during the period.

    d.   Added to the volume of units completed and transferred to finished goods during the period.

___ 4.   In a process cost system, costs flow from one departmental work in process account to the next in the same sequence as:

    a.   Selling and administrative costs are incurred.

    b.   Direct materials are purchased.

    c.   Payrolls are paid.

    d.   Actual units move through production.

___ 5.   A process cost system provides information useful for each of the following purposes *except*:

    a.   Determining a cost of goods sold figure to be reported in the balance sheet.

    b.   Identifying manufacturing inefficiencies.

    c.   Establishing selling prices.

    d.   Estimating future manufacturing costs.

___ 6.   Conversion costs equal the sum of:

    a.   direct labor costs and direct materials costs.

    b.   Direct materials costs and manufacturing overhead costs.

    c.   Manufacturing overhead costs and direct labor costs.

    d.   None of the above.

___ 7.   When expressed in terms of equivalent units, the resources needed to finish 500 units that are currently 25% complete, are approximately the same as the resources needed to:

    a.   start and finish 25 whole units from scratch.

    b.   start and finish 100 whole units from scratch.

    c.   start and finish 125 whole units from scratch.

    d.   start and finish 375 whole units from scratch.

___ 8.   When expressed in terms of equivalent units, the resources needed to start 500 units, but complete them only 25% of the way, are approximately the same as the resources needed to:

    a.   start and finish 25 whole units from scratch.

    b.   start and finish 100 whole units from scratch.

    c.   start and finish 125 whole units from scratch.

    d.   start and finish 375 whole units from scratch.

___ 9.   A company uses process costing system. It has two manufacturing processes: assembly and packaging. Which of the following journal entries is required to transfer costs from one production process to the next?

    a.   Debit Work in Process: Assembly; Credit Work in Process: Packaging.

    b.   Debit Work in Process: Packaging; Credit Work in Process: Assembly.

    c.   Debit Finished Goods; Credit Work in Process: Packaging.

    d.   Debit Finished Goods; Credit Work in Process: Assembly.

___ 10.   Which of the following is *not* part of a detailed production report used in most process costing environments?

    a.   The flow of physical goods for the period.

    b.   The number of equivalent units consumed during the period.

    c.   The cost per equivalent unit consumed during the period.

    d.   The total cost of goods sold for the period.

Exercises

1.   Listed below are six technical accounting terms emphasized in this chapter.

Conversion costs	*Equivalent units*
Job order costing	*Cost accounting systems*
Process costing	*Production cost report*

Each of the following statements may (or may not) describe one of these technical terms. In the space provided below each statement, indicate the accounting term described, or answer "None" if the statement does not correctly describe any of the terms.

a.   A summary that includes the periodic flow of physical goods through various phases of production.

    _____

b.   The account debited as costs are transferred out of the final Work in Process account.

    _____

c.   A measure of resources consumed during an accounting period expressed in whole units of production.

_____

d.   The cost accounting method used most in the continuous production of identical goods.

_____

e.   The cost accounting method likely to be used by companies who perform unique services for their clients.

_____

f.   The term used for the sum of direct materials and manufacturing overhead costs.

_____

2.   Winchester Company uses a process cost system. At the beginning of March, the Materials Inventory account showed a balance of $14,000. During March, purchases of materials on account totaled $119,000, and materials requisitions totaled $122,000. Of the materials placed into production, $100,000 went to the Assembly Department, and $22,000 went to the Painting Department.

     a.   Record a summary journal entry for the purchase of materials during March:

     b.   Record a summary journal entry for materials placed into production during March:

     c.   The balance in the Materials Inventory account at the end of March is
$_____.

3.   On March 1, the Work in Process Inventory of Textron's Assembly Department consisted of 600 units that were 100% complete with respect to materials, and 70% complete with respect to both labor and manufacturing overhead.

During March 2,600 completed units were transferred out of the Assembly Department to the Packaging Department.

On March 31, 500 units remain in process in the Assembly Department. These units are 80% complete with respect to materials, and 40% complete with respect to labor and manufacturing overhead.

The manufacturing costs incurred during March amounted to $24,000 in materials, $11,900 in labor, and $35,700 in manufacturing overhead.

a. Compute the equivalent units of material, labor, and manufacturing overhead that were required to complete the 600 units in process on March 1.

Material: _____ equivalents units

Labor: _____ equivalents units

Overhead: _____ equivalents units

b. Compute the number of units started and completed in the Assembly Department during March.

c. Compute the equivalent units of material, labor, and manufacturing overhead that were required to start 500 units that remain in process on March 31.

Material: _____ equivalents units

Labor: _____ equivalents units

Overhead: _____ equivalents units

d. Using data computed in parts a, b, and c, complete the following table to determine the cost per equivalent unit in Mach for material, labor, and manufacturing overhead.

Work done in March	Materials	Conversion
Beginning Work in Process		
Units Started and Completed		
Ending Work in Process		
Total Equivalent Units		
Costs Incurred in March		
Costs per Equivalent Unit		

Solution to Chapter 18 Self-Test

True or False

1. **T** Manufacturing activities involving a continuous stream of identical products are well suited to a process cost system.

2. **T** Process cost systems account separately for the manufacturing costs incurred by each production department.

3. **F** It is not unusual for companies with diverse manufacturing processes to us both process and job order costing systems simultaneously.

4.   **T** Manufacturing overhead and direct labor costs may be lumped together when these costs are incurred uniformly throughout the production process.

5.   **F** In a process cost system, costs are transferred from one Work in Process account to the next in the same *sequence* as actual products flow through production. Only when a product has passed through each processing department are its costs transferred to finished goods.

6.   **T** Throughout the period, units are continuously processed, completed, and transferred to finished goods. The quantity of goods that remain in production at the end of each period represents only a small portion of a company's total output for the entire period.

7.   **T** Unit costs are determined by dividing total manufacturing costs for the period by the number of units completed and transferred to finished goods during the period, even if some units in process at the end of the period.

8.   **T** In a process cost system, the output of one department becomes an input of the next. As such, the units of output for each department are uniquely defined for each phase of the production process.

9.   **F** In addition to external reporting requirements, job and process cost systems provide information used in setting prices, evaluating efficiency, and forecasting future operating results.

10.   **F** The cost of goods sold is recorded as goods are sold and transferred out of finished goods inventory.

11.   **F** The Work in Process account from which costs are transferred from is credited, and the Work in Process account to which costs are being transferred is debited.

12.   **F** As costs are transferred from the final Work in Process account the account is credited and, in most cases, Finished Goods Inventory is debited.

13.   **T** To measure efficiency, manufacturing costs are expressed in terms of equivalent whole units produced.

14.   **T** When Work in Process inventories are relatively small in comparison to the total cost of goods manufactured during the period, companies often simply charge all manufacturing costs directly to the Finished Goods Inventory.

Completion Statements

1. Cost accounting systems. 2. Process costing. 3. Job order accounting. 4. Conversion costs.
5. Equivalent units. 6. Production report.

Multiple Choice

1.   Answer **a**—answers **b** and **c** would be more indicative of a job cost system. There is no limit on the number of processes or departments that a process cost system may have.

2.   Answer **c**—the amount used in the entry is determined from a job cost sheet in a job cost system, or from unit cost date in a process cost system.

3.   Answer **b**—in most operations, units pass through production very quickly. Thus, at any one point in time, the number of units in process is relatively small in comparison to the total output for an entire period.

4.   Answer **d**—as units pass through production, accumulated costs are transferred from one work in process account to the next. As units are completed, the cumulative costs of the last work in process account in the sequence are transferred to finished goods.

5. Answer **a**—the cost of goods sold figure is reported in the income statement, not the balance sheet.

6. Answer **c**—When incurred uniformly throughout the production process, direct labor and manufacturing overhead are often lumped together and are referred to as conversion costs.

7. Answer **d**—If 500 units are 25% complete, it takes 375 whole units of input resources to complete them (500 x 75%)

8. Answer **c**—If 500 units are 25% complete, it took 125 whole units of input resources to get them processed that far (500 x 25%)

9. Answer **b**—Assuming that units are assembled before they can be packaged, the Work in Process: Packaging account is debited, and the Work in Process: Assembly account is credited, as costs are transferred between them.

10. Answer **d** — A production report details the costs of production, but not the costs of goods actually sold.

Solutions to Exercise

1.
a. Production cost report.
b. None (The statement describes the Finished Goods Inventory account.)
c. Equivalent units.
d. Process costing.
e. Job order costing.
f. Conversion costs.

2.
a. Materials inventory 119,000
   Accounts Payable 119,000
   To record materials purchased in March.
b. Work in Process Inventory, Assembly 100,000
   Work in Process Inventory, Painting 22,000
   Materials Inventory 122,000
To record materials used in March.
c. $11,000 ($14,000 + $119,000 - $122,000)

3.
a. Material: 600 x 0% = 0 equivalent units
   Conversion: 600 x 30% = 180 equivalent units

b. Units transferred out   2,600
   Less: Units in beginning Work in Process   600
Units started and completed in March   2,000
Of the 2,000 units started and completed in March, 100% of the material labor, and overhead required to product them was added during March.

c. Material: 500 x 80% = <u>400 equivalent units</u>

Conversion 500 x 40% = <u>200 equivalent units</u>

d.

Work done in March	Materials	Conversion
Beginning Work in Process	0	180
Units Started and Completed	2,000	2,000
Ending Work in Process	400	200
Total Equivalent Units	2,400	2,380
Costs Incurred in March	$24,000	$47,600
Costs per Equivalent Unit	$10	$20

19

COSTING AND THE VALUE CHAIN

HIGHLIGHTS OF THE CHAPTER

1. The *value chain* is a set of activities and resources necessary to create and deliver products or services valued by a business customers. The details of each organization's value chain differ as a function of the goods and or services being delivered.

2. For most companies, the following components of the value chain apply: (1) research and development (R & D) and design activities, (2) Suppliers and production-related activities, (3) marketing and distribution activities, and (4) customer service activities.

3. *R & D and design activities* include the creation of ideas and the development of prototype products, processes, and services. *Supplier and production-related activities* include the procurement of raw materials and supplies and the activities needed to convert them into finished goods and services. *Marketing and distribution activities,* are designed to provide information to potential customers and make products and services accessible to customers. *Customer service activities* are those resources consumed by supporting the product or service after it has been sold to the customer.

4. Organizations attempt to identify and eliminate the *non-value-added activities* in their value chains. *Value-added activities* add to the product's or service's desirability in the eyes of the consumer. Non-value-added activities do not add to the product's (or service's) desirability. Thus, when an organization engages in non-value-added activities, it can decrease its costs, without influencing the desirability of its products or services, if all or some of its non-value-added activities can be eliminated.

5. In the previous two chapters, our analysis was concentrated only on the production phase of the value chain. However, resources are consumed across the entire value chain. Organizations attempt to minimize resource consumption at all points on the value chain while simultaneously providing products and services desired by customers. The procedures used to assess resource consumption across the value chain include: (1) activity-based management, (2) target costing, (3) just-in-time inventory procedures, and (4) total quality management.

6. In Chapter 17, we introduced activity-based costing (ABC). The basic procedures related to ABC included the following: (1) identify activities that consume resources, (2) create associated activity cost pools, (3) identify activity measures, and (4) devise an appropriate cost per unit of each activity identified. If any of the activities identified can be eliminated from the value chain without decreasing the desirability of the product or service, and without increasing the cost associated with the total value chain, then that activity is a non-value-added activity (and a candidate for elimination).

7. Using activity-based costing information to help reduce and eliminate non-value-added activities is referred to as *activity-based management*. Activity-based management includes the assessment of numerous value chain activities, including R & D, distribution, administration, finance, marketing, and customer service. In many organizations, these "period expenses" are more significant contributors to profitability than product costs.

8. ABC information must be created before activity-based management can occur. Using ABC figures provides a better understanding of the many activities that consume resources and the costs associated with those resources. In addition, having benchmark information about competitive practices can help a company identify non-value-added activities. Benchmark information can be in the form of industry studies, competitive outside bids, or internal

prototyping. Thus, ABC is a critical component of activity-based management, but managing the activities also requires benchmark information.

9. ***Target costing*** is a business process aimed at the earliest stages of new product and service development (before creation and design of production methods). It is a process driven by the customer, focused on design, and encompassing the entire life of the product. The objective of target costing is to provide an organization with a production process that provides adequate profits.

10. Target costing begins with the customer. Customer desires about functionality, quality, and price drive the analysis. Knowing customer requirements also means understanding competitor offerings. If a competitor offers a higher quality product with a similar functionality at a lower price, companies attempt to reengineer their production processes in response to competitive pressures.

11. At the most basic level, a desired target cost is the cost of resources that should be consumed to create a product that can be sold at a target price. The target price is determined through interaction with consumers and by considering acceptable margins of profit. The basic target cost formula is as follows:

Target Cost = Target Price – Profit Margin

12. Target costing can be understood by considering its four components: (1) planning and market analysis, (2) development, (3) production design, and (4) production. The latter two of these stages is where the achievement of the target cost occurs.

13. A final aspect of target costing is the consideration of product costs over the life of the product. ***Life-cycle costing*** is the consideration of all potential resources consumed by the product over its entire life. These costs stretch from product development and R & D through warranty and disposal costs. These additional product life-cycle considerations are a formal part of the target costing process.

14. The target costing process has several characteristics worth noting: (1) the entire value chain is involved in driving costs down while satisfying customer needs, (2) a clear outstanding of the connection between key component processes and associated costs is essential, (3) target costing involves an emphasis on a product's functional characteristics and the importance of these characteristics to the customer, (4) a primary objective of target costing is to reduce development time, and (5) ABC information is very useful in determining which process changes will drive out costs associated with the activities necessary to achieve the target cost.

15. One approach used to drive cost out of the production process is a ***just-in-time (JIT) manufacturing system***. The phrase "just in time" refers to acquiring materials and manufacturing goods only as needed to fill customer orders. JIT systems are sometimes described as ***demand pull*** manufacturing because production is totally driven by customer demand. This contrasts with more traditional ***supply push*** systems in which manufacturers produce as many goods as possible.

16. A JIT system is characterized by extremely small or nonexistent inventories of materials, work in process, and finished goods. Materials are scheduled to arrive only as needed, and products flow quickly from one production process to the next without having to move into temporary storage facilities. Finished goods in excess of existing customer orders are not produced.

17. Storing inventory can be costly and lead to liquidity problems. One goal of JIT is to reduce or eliminate costs associated with storing inventory, most of which do ***not add value*** to the product. JIT is much more than an approach to inventory management, however. It is a philosophy of eliminating non-value-adding activities and increasing product quality throughout the manufacturing process.

18. Perhaps the most important goal of a successful JIT system is to control costs without sacrificing product quality. This goal is achieved, in part, by cultivating strong and lasting relationships with

a limited number of select suppliers. It is important to understand that reliable vendor relationships are essential for achieving long-term quality, even if the prices charged are not the lowest possible.

19. Implementing a successful JIT system also involves a commitment to achieve *zero defects*. This commitment requires that quality be designed-in and manufactured-in, rather than achieved by inspecting out defective products at the end of the manufacturing process. Therefore, in a JIT system, products must be designed in a manner that simplifies the manufacturing process and reduces the risk of defects.

20. Workers in a JIT system must be extremely versatile. Since products are produced only as needed, workers, must be able to shift quickly from the production of one product to another. To do so, they often must learn to perform various tasks and to operate different machines. Many companies have found that this concept of *flexible manufacturing* increases employee morale, skill and productivity.

21. To accommodate the demands of flexible manufacturing within a JIT system, an efficient plant layout is critical. Machines used in sequential order must be located in close proximity to each other in order to achieve a smooth and rapid flow of work in process. Since machinery downtime can interrupt the entire production process, equipment reliability is also a vital concern. To help ensure reliability, workers in a JIT system are often trained to perform *preventive maintenance* on the machinery they use and to make many routine repairs themselves.

22. Efficient JIT systems are designed to avoid bottlenecks and to ensure that jobs are completed "just in time" for delivery to the customer. Thus, an important aspect of JIT efficiency is *cycle time*. Cycle time is often viewed as containing four separate elements: (1) processing time, (2) storage and waiting time, (3) movement time, and (4) inspection time. Only during *processing time*, however, is value added to the product. Ideally, the other elements should be reduced as much as possible.

23. A widely used measure of JIT efficiency is the *manufacturing efficiency ratio*. This measure (sometimes called the "throughput ratio") expresses the time spent in value-added activities (processing activities) as percentage of total cycle time. Thus, the ratio is calculated by dividing value-added time by total cycle time. The primary purpose of the ratio is to highlight the percentage of time spent engaged in non-value-added activities. The optimal efficiency ratio is 100%, which indicates no time spent on non-value-added activities. In practice, however, this ratio is often considerably *less than 100%.*

24. Accounting systems in JIT companies also measure product *quality*. One widely used measure of production quality is expressed in terms of *defects per million units produced* (or in defects per thousand units produced). In some companies, defect rates have been reduced to less than one defective unit per million units of production. Other measures of quality may include merchandise returns, warranty claims processed, customer complaints, and the results of customer satisfaction surveys. JIT does not, in itself, ensure quality. Rather, it establishes *striving for quality* as a basic goal of the organization.

25. JIT systems are *not appropriate for all companies*. If a company does not have access to highly reliable sources of supply, it needs to maintain reasonable levels of materials inventories. Likewise, if a company has a lengthy cycle time, or if it cannot achieve a nearly zero-defects level of production, it should consider maintaining an adequate level of finished goods inventory to ensure prompt deliveries to customers. All companies can benefit, however, from the basic philosophy of the JIT approach, which is *striving to eliminate inefficiency and to improve product quality.*

26. The adoption of JIT techniques demonstrates that the current global competitive market requires that firms compete on quality and costs. The International Organization for Standardization has developed quality standards referred to as *ISO 9000*. These standards identify quality guidelines

for design development, production, inspection, and servicing of products and services. Many purchasers of goods and services require the supplier to be "ISO 9000 certified." The U. S. auto manufacturers have developed their own similar set of standards *QSO 9000*, and require their suppliers to have this quality certification.

27.   The cost of ignoring quality can be very high. Companies that are able to compete globally on quality and costs inevitably have well-developed *total quality management (TQM)* processes. *TQM* includes assigning responsibility for managing quality, and evaluating and rewarding quality performance. Accountants participate in this measurement and reporting process by designing systems that track quality and assign costs to quality failures.

28.   Four components of quality are typically considered when designing a measurement system to track quality failure costs: (1) *Prevention costs* refer to the resources consumed in activities that prevent defects from occurring, (2) *appraisal costs* are incurred to ensure that products conform to quality standards, (3) *internal failure costs* include additional production-related costs incurred to correct low-quality output, (4) *external failure costs* are incurred because quality failures are allowed to enter the market. These four types of quality costs are not independent. If, for example, more time and effort are spent ensuring that defective goods are not shipped to customers, lower external failure costs are likely.

29.   Measuring quality without concern for productivity can be a recipe for bankruptcy, Quality and productivity are linked, and managers would naturally prefer to undertake activities that reduce the failure costs associated with low quality and increase productivity. Fortunately, this often *is possible*. Managers frequently find that activities that reduce scrap and the need to rework manufactured items also increase productivity.

30.   We have identified four techniques commonly used by organization to manager costs across the value chain. (1) activity-based management, (2) target costing, (3) just-in-time, and (4) total quality management. The underlying objective of these four techniques is to *eliminate non-value-added activities* from the value chain. This objective is achieved by assigning employees the responsibility for managing these non-value added activities, providing information, about the cost of these activities, and rewarding managers who eliminate these activities. The customer ultimately defines non-value-added activities. It is true that in determining the shape and structure of the value chain, the customer is king.

TEST YOURSELF ON MANAGING ACROSS THE VALUE CHAIN

True or False

For each of the following statements, circle the T or the F to indicate whether the statement is true or false.

T   F   1.   Activity-based management is the term used to describe the set of activities and resources necessary to create and deliver a product or service valued by customers.

T   F   2.   It is usually beneficial for organization to eliminate all non-value-added activities in their value chain.

T   F   3.   The process of using activity-based costing to help reduce or eliminate non-value-added activities is referred to as benchmarking.

T F 4. Activity-based costing information is often very useful in assessing the activities associated with non-production-related costs such as R & D, distribution, administration, marketing, and customer service.

T F 5. The need for benchmarking data is virtually eliminated when a successful activity-based management system is in place.

T F 6. Target costing is a business practice aimed at the final stages of production, after the creation and design of production methods.

T F 7. Target costing begins with the understanding of customer needs.

T F 8. The target costing formula sets the target cost equal to the target price plus an agreed upon profit margin by management.

T F 9. The determination of the least costly combination of resources to create a particular product is referred to as research and development (R & D).

T F 10. The consideration of all potential resources consumed by a product over its entire life is referred to as life-cycle costing.

T F 11. A primary objective of target costing is to increase development time while decreasing defective units of production.

T F 12. Just-in-time (JIT) systems are sometimes referred to as supply push manufacturing because production is totally driven by the need to supply customers "just in time" with the goods that they demand.

T F 13. Just-in-time (JIT) systems are characterized by extremely small or nonexistent inventories.

T F 14. Perhaps the most important goal of a successful JIT system is to control product costs without sacrificing product quality.

T F 15. The cost of raw materials should always be the determining factor in selecting a supplier.

T F 16. To achieve a goal of zero defects, resources must be consumed to perform rigid quality control inspections.

T F 17. To help ensure equipment reliability, workers in a JIT system are often trained to perform preventive maintenance on the machinery they use.

T F 18. The length of time required for a product to pass completely through a manufacturing process is called the efficiency ratio.

T F 19. The manufacturing efficiency ratio is computed by dividing value-added time by non-value-added time.

T F 20. Most companies have manufacturing efficiency ratios of considerably less than 100%.

T F 21. A commonly reported measure of cost efficiency is stated in terms of defective units per million.

T F 22. When implemented properly, a JIT system ensures product quality.

T F 23. The maintenance of near-zero levels of inventory is advantageous for virtually all companies, large and small.

T F 24. Prevention costs are not independent of external failure costs.

T F 25. It is virtually impossible to reduce the failure costs associated with low quality while, at the same time, increase productivity.

Completion Statements

Fill in the necessary word to complete the following statements:

1. A _____ is the linked set of activities and resources necessary to create and deliver products or services to customers.

2. Organizations attempt to identify and eliminate the _____-_____-_____ activities in their value chains.

3. _____-_____ activities contribute to a product's or service's desirability in the eyes of the consumer.

4. The process of using activity-based costing information to help reduce or eliminate non-value-added activities is referred to as _____-_____ _____.

5. _____ _____ is a business process aimed at the earliest stages of new product or service development, before creation and design of production methods.

6. The process of determining the least costing combination of resources to create a product desired by the customer is called _____ _____.

7. _____-_____ _____ is the consideration of all potential resources consumed by a product over its entire life.

8. _____-_____-_____ manufacturing systems are sometimes referred to as "demand pull" systems.

9. The _____ _____ _____ is computed by dividing value-added time by total cycle time.

10. The length of time required for a product to pass completely through a manufacturing process is called the _____ _____.

11. The International Organization for Standardization has developed quality standards referred to as _____ _____.

12. The assigning of responsibility for managing quality, providing good quality measures for decision making, and rewarding quality performance is referred to as _____ _____ _____.

Multiple Choice

Choose the best answer for each of the following questions and enter the identifying letter in the space provided.

___ 1. Which of the following is *not* considered an active component of the value chain?
    a. Research and development and design activities.
    b. Marketing and distribution activities.
    c. Non-value added activities.
    d. Customer service activities.

___ 2. Which of the following would be considered a value-added activity:
    a. The storage of raw materials inventory.
    b. The use of high quality materials in manufacturing products.
    c. The moving of units from work in process to a finished goods warehouse.
    d. The hiring of security personnel to guard a raw materials warehouse.

___ 3. The process of using activity-based costs to help reduce or eliminate non-value-added activities is called:
    a. Activity-based management.
    b. Activity-based costing.
    c. Activity-based benchmarking.
    d. Activity-based elimination.

___ 4. Which of the following is a component of activity-based management, but is not a component of activity-based costing?
    a. Identify activities.
    b. Identify activity measures.
    c. Analyze activities.
    d. Determine cost per unit of activity.

5. The primary objective of target costing is to:
   a. Provide and organization with a production process that pleases the customer and results in adequate profits.
   b. Identify non-value-added activities.
   c. Identify value-added activities.
   d. Improve product quality.

6. The target cost formula is stated as follows:
   a. Target Cost = Target Price – Non-Value-Added Activities.
   b. Target Cost = Target Price + Value -Added Activities.
   c. Target Cost = Target Price – Profit Margin.
   d. Target Cost = Target Price + Profit Margin.

7. Which of the following is *not* a characteristic of the target costing process?
   a. Reducing costs while satisfying customer needs.
   b. Understanding the connection between key components of the production process and costs.
   c. Emphasizing a product's functional characteristics and their importance to the customer.
   d. Increasing development time in order to improve the desirability of products in the eyes of the customer.

8. Which of the following is *not* a characteristic of just-in-time manufacturing systems?
   a. Reduced inventory levels.
   b. Production output described as "supply push" manufacturing.
   c. Close relationships with suppliers.
   d. Highly skilled work force.

9. To achieve "zero defects," a manufacturing firm must:
   a. Implement flexible manufacturing.
   b. Increase quality control inspections.
   c. Obtain raw material at the lowest prices possible and invest and the savings in more stringent quality control measures.
   d. Consider design and manufacturing processes as part of a total quality management program.

10. Which of the following is *not* considered a component of a flexible manufacturing environment?
   a. Efficient plant layouts.
   b. Reliable equipment.
   c. Workers trained, at the highest levels of professionalism, to perform one task extremely well.
   d. Workers trained to conduct preventive maintenance on machinery.

_ 11. Which of the following is *not* considered an element of total cycle time?
    a. Design and development time.

    b. Processing time.

    c. Storage and waiting time.

    d. Inspection time.

_ 12. Of total cycle time, value-added activities occur only during:
    a. Design and development time.

    b. Processing time.

    c. Storage and waiting time.

    d. Inspection time.

_ 13. A companies total cycle time is 40 hours. Of this time, 30 hours represent non-value-added activities. The company's manufacturing efficiency ratio (expressed as a percentage) is:
    a. 25%.

    b. 10%.

    c. 75%.

    d. 30%.

_ 14. Which of the following is *not* considered a cost component of achieving quality?
    a. Prevention costs.

    b. Appraisal costs.

    c. Activity-based costs.

    d. External failure costs.

Exercises

1. Listed below are eight technical accounting terms emphasized in this chapter.

Value chain	*Value-added activities*
Activity-based management	*Target costing*
Life-cycle costing	*Just-in-time manufacturing*
Manufacturing efficiency ratio	*Cycle time*

Each of the following statements may (or may not) describe one of these technical terms. In the space provided below each statement, indicate the accounting term described, or answer "None" if the statement does not correctly describe any of the terms.

a. The process of using activity-based costs to help reduce or eliminate non-value added activities.

_____

b.   The length of time for a product to pass completely through the entire manufacturing process.

_____

c.   An approach to manufacturing that reduces or eliminates non-value-added activities, such as the maintenance of inventories.

_____

d.   The consideration of all potential resources consumed by a product over its entire life.

_____

e.   Processing time stated as a percentage of total cycle time.

_____

f.   An activity in the value chain that does not increase the desirability of a firm's product or services in the eyes of the customer.

_____

g.   A business process aimed at the earliest stages of product or service development, before the creation and design of production methods.

_____

h.   The set activities necessary to create and distribute a desirable product or service to the customer.

_____

2.   The following quality-related items fall into one of four cost classifications. In the space next to each item, indicate its classification using the appropriate letter **P, A, I,** or **E** as shown below:

P   Prevention costs.
A   Appraisal. costs.
I   Internal failure costs.
E   External failure costs.

a.   ____   Resources consumed to inspect materials.

b.   ____   Resources consumed in quality training activities.

c.   ____   Resources consumed related to product warranties.

d.   ____   Resources consumed to inspect finished products.

e.   ____   Resources consumed to rework defective units.

f.   ____   Resources consumed to dispose of scrap and waste.

3.   Bruns Corporation recently hired a consultant to study its cycle time requirements. The consultant provided Bruns with the following reports:

	Hours Required
Set-up time	1
Storage of materials	28
Cutting materials	8
Bending materials	5
Assembling finished products	7
Moving finished goods to warehouse	1

Based on the report shown above, answer the following questions:

a.   The company's total cycle time is: _____

b.   The company's manufacturing efficiency ratio is: _____

c.   List the company's value-added activities.

SOLUTIONS TO CHAPTER 19 SELF-TEST

True or False

1.   **F** The *value chain* is the term used to describe the set of activities and resources necessary to create and deliver a product or service valued by customers.

2.   **T** When an organization consumes non-value-added resources, it can decrease costs if the activities that consume these resources can be eliminated without changing the desirability of the products being produced.

3.   **F** The process of using activity-based costing to help reduce or eliminate non-value-added activities is referred to as *activity-based management*.

4.   **T** In many organizations, these "period expenses" often play a greater role in the determination of profitability than product costs.

5.   **F** Benchmark information about competitive practices can help a company identify non-value-added activities. Benchmark information can be in the form of industry studies, competitive outside bids, or internal prototyping.

6.   **F** Target costing is a business process aimed at the *earliest* stages of new product development, before the creation and design of production methods.

7.   **T** Target costing begins with understanding customer desires about quality, functionality, and price sensitivity.

8.   **F** The target costing formula sets the target cost equal to the target price *minus* an agreed upon profit margin by management.

9.   **F** The determination of the least costly combination of resources to create a particular product is referred to as *value engineering*.

10.   **T** Life-cycle costs stretch from product development and R & D costs through warranty and disposal costs. Product life-cycle costs are a part of the target costing process.

11.   **F** A primary object of target costing is to *decrease* product development time.

12. **F** JIT systems are sometimes referred to as ***demand pull*** manufacturing because production is totally driven by customer demand.

13. **T** JIT systems are characterized by extremely small or nonexistent inventories of materials, work in process, and finished goods.

14. **T** A central goal of a successful JIT system is to control product costs without sacrificing product quality. This goal is achieved, in part, by cultivating strong and lasting relationships with a limited number of select suppliers.

15. **F** If quality is a goal, the cost of raw materials should ***not*** be a determining factor in selecting a supplier. In fact, slightly higher prices may actually result in quality improvement and cost savings in the long-run.

16. **F** To achieve a goal of zero defects, quality must be achieved ***during*** the production process rather than be achieved by inspecting products at the ***end*** of the manufacturing process.

17. **T** Since machinery downtime can interrupt the entire production process, equipment reliability is a vital concern. To help ensure equipment reliability, workers, in a JIT system are often trained to perform preventive maintenance on the machinery they use.

18. **F** The length of time required for a product to pass completely through a manufacturing process is called the ***cycle time***.

19. **F** The manufacturing efficiency ratio is computed by dividing value-added time by the ***cycle time***.

20. **T** The ***optimal*** manufacturing efficiency ratio is 100%. In practice, however, this ratio is always considerably less than 100%.

21. **F** A commonly reported measure of ***product quality*** is stated in terms of defective units per million.

22. **F** A JIT system does not, in itself, ensure quality. Rather, it ***establishes striving for quality*** as a basic goal of the organization.

23. **F** The maintenance of near-zero inventories is ***not*** appropriate for all companies. If a company does not have access to highly reliable sources of supply, it should maintain reasonable inventories of raw materials. Likewise, if its cycle time is lengthy, or it cannot achieve a nearly zero defects level of production, it should consider maintaining adequate levels of finished goods inventory to ensure prompt deliver of quality goods to its customers.

24. **T** If more resources are consumed in preventing defective goods from leaving the firm, lower external failure costs are likely to be incurred. Thus, prevention costs and external failure costs are not independent.

25. **F** Managers often find that by reducing the costs associated with low quality, productivity is increased. For example, activities that reduce the need to rework defect units often times increase productivity and throughput.

Completion Statements

1. Value chain 2. Non-value-added. 3. Value-added. 4. Activity-based management. 5. Target costing. 6. Value engineering. 7. Life-cycle costing. 8. Just-in-time. 9. Manufacturing efficiency ratio. 10. Cycle time. 11. ISO 9000 12. Total quality management.

Multiple Choice

1. Answer **c**—The elimination of non-value-added activities is an important aspect of managing a firm's value chain. Non-value-added activities themselves, however, are not considered active components of the value chain.

2. Answer **b**—Value-added activities add to a product's desirability in the eyes of the customer. Having a product that was manufactured using high quality materials is desirable to most consumers. The storage of inventory, the moving of finished goods, and the guarding of a warehouse do nothing to improve a product's desirability.

3. Answer **a**—Activity-based management is the term used to describe the reduction or elimination of non-value-added activities. Activity-based costing is a process by which costs are assigned to products based upon measurable activity levels (both value-added and non-value-added activities).

4. Answer **c**—Activity-based costing is a subset of activity-based management. Thus, activity-based management includes *all* of the components of activity-based costing, but activity-based costing does *not* include all of the components of activity-based management. Activity-based costing and activity based management both include the identification of activities, the identification of activity measures, and the determination of cost per unit of activity. Only activity-based management, however, includes the detailed analysis of activities.

5. Answer **a**—Target costing may involve the identification of value-added and non-value-added activities, and it certainly takes into consideration product quality. It's primary objective, however, is to develop a production process that pleases the customer and results in adequate profits for the company.

6. Answer **c**—The target price, minus the target cost, is the company's desired profit margin. Thus, the target cost equals the target price minus the desired profit margin.

7. Answer **d**—Target costing stresses the ***reduction*** of development time. The cross-functional, cross-organizational team approach of target costing allows for simultaneous, rather than sequential, consideration of solutions to development concerns, thus enabling a company to speed up its development time.

8. Answer **b**—JIT systems are sometimes described as ***demand pull*** manufacturing because production is totally driven by customer demand. This contrasts with more traditionally "supply push" systems in which manufacturers simply product at maximum, or near maximum, levels of output. Reduced inventories, close relationships with suppliers, and a highly skilled work force are all essential characteristics of a successful JIT system.

9. Answer **d**—To achieve a goal of zero defects, quality must be designed-in and manufactured-in, rather than achieved by inspecting-out defective products at the ***end*** of the manufacturing process.

10. Answer **c**—In JIT environment, workers must be extremely versatile. Since are produced only as needed, workers must be able to shift quickly from the production of one product to another. To do so, they must learn to perform various tasks and to operate difference machines. Many companies have found that this concept of "flexible manufacturing" increases employee morale, skill, and productivity.

11. Answer **a**—Cycle time includes those elements of production which occur ***after*** a product or manufacturing process has been developed and designed. The four elements of cycle time include: (1) processing time, (2) storage and waiting time, (3) movement time, and (4) inspection time.

12. Answer **b**—Only during processing time is value added to the product. Ideally, the other elements of a product's cycle time (see solution 11 above) should be reduced as much as possible.

13. Answer ***a***—The manufacturing efficiency ratio is computed by dividing ***value-added*** time by the total cycle time. If a company's total cycle time is 40 hours, and its non-value-added time is 30 hours, then value-added time is 10 hours (40 hours – 30 hours). Thus, the company's manufacturing efficiency ratio is 25% (10 hours ÷ 40 hours = 25%).

14.   Answer **c**—The four components of the cost of quality are: (1) prevention costs, (2) appraisal costs, (3) internal failure costs, and (4) external failure costs. All of these costs might be associated with various activities identified in an activity-based costing system.

Solutions to Exercises

1.

    a.   Activity-based management
    b.   Cycle time
    c.   Just-in-time manufacturing
    d.   Life-cycle costing
    e.   Manufacturing efficiency ratio
    f.   None (This statement describes non-value-added activities.)
    g.   Target costing
    h.   Value chain

2.

    a.   A
    b.   P
    c.   E
    d.   A
    e.   I
    f.   I

3.

    a.   50 Hours (the total time required for all activities listed in the report)
    b.   40% [(8 hours + 5 hours + 7 hours) ÷ 50 hours)]
    c.   Cutting materials, bending materials, and assembling finished products.

20

COST-VOLUME-PROFIT ANALYSIS

HIGHLIGHTS OF THE CHAPTER

1. *Cost-volume-profit analysis* is a *predictive tool* used by managers to plan and control the activities of a business. With this tool, management can forecast future costs, revenues, and profits at *various levels* of business activity.

2. Some questions answered by cost-volume-profit analysis include: What level of sales must be reached in order to break even? What will happen to net income if unit selling prices are reduced by $1 and unit volume increases by 10%? etc. These types of questions can be answered by understanding relationships among revenues, costs, and estimated unit sales volume.

3. The first step in cost-volume-profit analysis is to know *how costs behave* in response to changes in some activity. Therefore, we must determine a measurable business activity to serve as a *cost driver*. A cost driver is an activity having a strong influence over the amount of costs a business incurs. The activity selected is called the activity base. An *activity base* may be an input to the production process (such as direct labor hours or machine-hours), or an output measure (such as unit sales or total revenue)

4. There are three general types of cost behavior: (1) fixed costs, (2) variable costs, and (3) semivariable costs (or mixed costs). To illustrate these behaviors, we will examine the costs incurred to operate an automobile using *miles driven* as in activity base.

a. *Fixed costs* do not vary in response to changes in the activity base. For example, an automobile's annual registration and insurance are fixed costs that do not change in response to total miles driven during the year. Thus, if your annual registration and insurance costs total $1,000, this is the amount that must be paid regardless of how many miles you drive. It is important to note that that *average* fixed cost per unit of activity base *does* change as units of the activity base change. For instance, if you drive your car 10,000 miles in a given year, the average fixed costs per mile for registration and insurance amounts to ten cents per mile ($1,000 ÷ 10,000 miles). If, however, your drive your car only 5,000 miles during the year, average fixed costs per mile would *increase* to twenty cents per mile ($1,000 ÷ 5,000 miles). Of course, if drive a total of 20,000 miles during the year, average fixed costs per mile would *decrease* to five cents per mile ($1,000 ÷ 20,000 miles).

b. *Variable costs* are those that, *in total*, increase and decrease in *direct proportion* to changes in the activity base. The cost of gasoline is a variable cost related to the operation of your automobile. The more miles you drive your car during the year, the *higher* your total variable cost for gasoline will be. Likewise, if you put only a few miles on your car during the year, your total variable cost for gasoline will be relatively low. It is important to note that only total variable costs vary in response to changes in the activity base. The *average variable cost per unit* of activity base *does not change* significantly in response to changes in the activity base. Thus, regardless of how many miles your drive your car during the year, the average cost of gasoline consumed for *each mile* driven remains, for all practical purposes, *constant*.

c. *Semivariable costs (or mixed costs)* are those costs that include *both* fixed and variable elements. The fixed component represents some minimum level of cost incurred regardless of the activity base volume. Beyond that minimum costs vary in proportion to changes in the activity base levels. Assuming that a minimum amount of maintenance is required regardless of how many miles your drive each year, repair costs constitute a semivariable cost of operating your automobile. During years in which you drive relatively few miles, your total maintenance costs will probably not exceed the minimum. However, during those years in which you travel a great deal, total maintenance costs can be expected to exceed the minimum significantly.

5.   A technique examined in the chapter for determining the fixed and variable elements of semivariable costs is called the **high-low method**. This technique examines the change in cost corresponding to the highest and the lowest levels of activity base volume.

6.   By combining all variable, semivariable, and fixed costs, we may formulate and state a **cost formula** for a business. For instance, a cost formula for an automobile might reveal that "it costs $900 per year plus 20 cents per mile to operate." The $900 represents the total of all fixed costs, including the fixed portion of all semivariable costs. The 20 cents per mile represents the variable operation cost per mile, which includes the variable portion of all semivariable costs.

7.   **Average unit cost** is the total manufacturing cost of the period divided by the units of output produced. Within certain limits, average unit cost tends to decrease as output increases because the fixed manufacturing costs are being spread over more units.

8.   The **relevant range** is the range of volume levels (or production levels) over which assumptions made about cost-volume-profit relationships remain valid.

9.   Cost-volume relationships may be expressed graphically with dollar cost as the vertical axis and volume as the horizontal axis.

10.   By plotting both costs and revenues at various levels of volume on the same graph, a **cost-volume-profit graph** may be developed which illustrates the expected profit or loss at any level of volume.

11.   The intersection of the total revenue line with the total cost line on a cost-volume-profit graph (where profit equals zero) is called the **break-even point**. The slope of the total revenue line equals the **average selling price** per unit of activity base. The slope of the total cost line equals the **average variable cost** per unit of activity base. The difference between these two slopes (i.e. average unit selling price minus average unit variable cost) is referred to as the contribution margin.

12.   A key relationship in cost-volume-profit analysis is the **contribution margin**. The contribution margin is what remains after subtracting variable costs from sales. Contribution margin may be expressed as total sales minus total variable costs, or on a per-unit basis as the unit sales price minus variable costs per unit.

13.   When the contribution margin is expressed as a **percentage of sales**, its is called the **contribution margin ratio**. On a per-unit basis, the ratio is computed as follows:

$$\frac{\text{Unit Contribution Margin}}{\text{Sales Price}}$$

14.   The contribution margin may be used to compute the sales volume required to break even or to earn a desired level of operating income. The required sales volume **in units** may be computed as follows:

$$\frac{\text{Fixed Costs} + \text{Operating Income}}{\text{Contribution Margin per Unit}}$$

To find the required sales volume stated in dollars, the formula is modified as shown below:

$$\frac{\text{Fixed Costs} + \text{Operating Income}}{\text{Contribution Margin Ratio}}$$

15.   The dollar amount by which actual sales volume is expected to exceed the break-even point is called the **margin of safety**. The margin of safety provides a quick means of estimating a company's operating income at any sales level above the break-even point. The estimated operating income may be estimated as follows:

Margin of Safety x Contribution Margin Ratio

16.　The contribution margin ratio may also be used to *estimate* the change in operating income likely to result from any expected change in sales volume. The change in operating income can be determined as follows:

Change in Sales Volume x Contribution Margin Ratio

17.　Cost-volume-profit relationships are widely used as companies formulate budgets, make planning decisions, and develop marketing strategies.

18.　The higher the contribution margin ratio, the lower the dollar sales volume needed to cover fixed expenses and to provide a given level of operating income. At any given sales level, *selling products with high contribution margin ratios is more profitable than selling products with low contribution margin ratios*. Thus sales resulting in high contribution margin ratios are said to be *high quality* sales.

19.　Cost-volume-profit analysis is most often concerned with *operating income* as opposed to *net income*, as income tax expense is neither fixed nor a variable cost.

20.　In a cost-volume-profit analysis, the following simplifying assumptions must be made: (a) unit sales prices remain constant, (b) the sales mix of products remains constant, (c) fixed expenses remain constant, (d) variable costs remain a constant percentage of sales revenue, and (e) the number of units produced during the period equals the number of units sold.

21.　The use of cost-volume profit analysis is not limited to accountants. On the contrary, it provides valuable information to many individuals throughout an organization. For instance, cost-volume-profit relationships are widely used during the budget process to set sales targets, estimate costs, and to provide information for a variety of budgetary decisions.

TEST YOURSELF ON COST-VOLUME-PROFIT ANALYSIS

True or False

For each of the following statements, circle the T or the F to indicate whether the statement is true or false.

T　F　1.　Cost-volume-profit analysis is a means of determining the costs incurred, and the revenue earned, in prior accounting periods.

T　F　2.　When cost-volume-profit analysis is used, the need for planning and budgeting is greatly reduced.

T　F　3.　An activity base can be based upon units of input or upon units of output.

T　F　4.　When products are handmade, direct labor is most likely considered a variable cost.

T　F　5.　A semivariable (or "mixed") cost is one that is partially tax deductible and partially nondeductible.

T　F　6.　The property taxes paid on a factory are fixed costs.

T　F　7.　Direct costs are generally fixed costs.

T　F　8.　Indirect costs (for example, manufacturing overhead) are always fixed costs.

T　F　9.　Variable costs vary in direct proportion to changes in the activity base.

T F 10. Assume that the annual cost of operating a tractor is $3,000 plus 90 cents per mile. Thus, the semivariable cost is $3,000 and the variable cost is 90 cents per mile.

T F 11. Cost-volume relationships do not necessarily hold true outside of the relevant range.

T F 12. If item A has a higher contribution margin than item B, it must also have a higher contribution margin ratio than item B.

T F 13. The break-even point on a cost-volume profit graph corresponds to the level of volume at which total revenue equals total variable costs.

T F 14. If a business has a $100,000 margin of safety, the business will still be profitable unless net income declines by more than $100,000.

T F 15. A cost-volume-profit graph includes both revenue and total cost projections.

T F 16. In cost-volume-profit analysis, "profit" generally refers to operating income.

Completion Statements

Fill in the necessary word to complete the following statements:

1. Direct labor and fuel consumption are examples of _____ costs, while plant security and property taxes are examples of _____ costs.

2. Miles drive is an example of a (an) _____ _____ which could be used in analyzing the cost of operating an automobile.

3. Semivariable costs are also called _____ costs and have both a(an) _____ portion representing a minimum level of cost and a(an) _____ portion that responds to changes in volume.

4. The cost of producing bottled beer for the Green Beer Company is $2 million plus 5 cents per bottle. If 10 million bottles are produced, the _____ costs will be $500,000, the _____ costs will be $2 million, and the average cost per bottle will be $_____.

5. The dollar amount by which the sales price of a unit exceeds the variable costs relating to the unit is called the _____ _____.

6. The contribution margin ratio is the percentage of each _____ dollar that covers the _____ _____ of a business and adds to the _____ _____ of the business.

7. Product X sells for $5 per unit and requires variable expenses of $2 per unit. Product Y sells for $10 per unit and requires variable expenses of $4.70 per unit. For Product X, the contribution margin is $_____ and the contribution ratio is _____. For product Y, the contribution margin is $_____ and the contribution margin ratio is _____.

8. Referring to Question 7, assume that the total fixed costs to produce either product are the same. If total dollar sales are expected to be the same no matter which product is produced and sold, it would be more profitable to produce product _____.

9. The margin of safety is the amount by which total dollar _____could _____ and still allow a business to _____ _____.

Multiple Choice

Choose the best answer for each of the following questions and enter the identifying letter in the space provided.

___ 1. The following information would be used to determine the unit cost per item sold:
   a. Selling price per unit.

   b. Total dollar sales.

   c. Total unit sales.

   d. None of the above.

___ 2. Which of the following average costs per unit will usually decrease by the greatest percentage with an increase in the volume of units produced?
   a. Average fixed cost per unit.

   b. Average semivariable costs per unit.

   c. Average variable cost per unit.

   d. Average total cost per unit.

___ 3. Within the relevant range of production, average variable costs *per unit* will tend to:
   a. Vary inversely with the level of production.

   b. Remain relatively constant.

   c. Vary in direct proportion with the level of production.

   d. Fluctuate drastically.

___ 4. The high and low levels of direct-labor hours and total manufacturing overhead of Kelly's Mfg. Co. are shown below:

	Direct Labor-Hours	Total Manufacturing Overhead
Highest level	4,000	$12,000
Lowest level	1,000	6,000

Kelly's fixed portion of total manufacturing overhead is approximately:
   a. $8,000.

   b. $4,000.

   c. $2 per direct labor-hour.

   d. $4,000 plus $2 direct labor-hour.

5. When a cost-volume-profit graph is prepared, the break-even point will always be found:

    a.   At 50% of normal capacity.

    b.   At the volume resulting in the lowest average unit cost.

    c.   At a volume where total revenue equals total fixed costs.

    d.   At a volume where total revenue equals total fixed costs plus total variable costs.

6. Which of the following assumptions is *not* made in the analysis of a cost-volume-profit graph?

    a.   The unit sales price remains constant.

    b.   Variable expenses per unit increase in proportion to changes in sales volume.

    c.   Fixed expenses remain constant at all levels of production within the relevant range.

    d.   If more than one product is produced and sold, the sales mix remains constant.

7. The contribution margins of product A and product B are $7 and $6, respectively. Total fixed expenses are the same when either item is produced. Which of the following statements will always be true?

    a.   The contribution margin ratio is higher for product A than for product B.

    b.   If the company decided to produce only one product, the break-even point in units would be lower for product A than for product B.

    c.   The contribution margin per direct labor hour is higher for product A than for product B.

    d.   If sales will be $600,000 no matter which product sold, it will be more profitable to sell product A than product B.

8. Super-Duper Glue sells for $2.00 per tube and has related variable expenses of $1.20 per tube. The fixed expenses of producing Super Duper Glue are $48,000 per month. How many tubes of glue must be sold each month for a monthly operating income of $60,000?

    a.   45,000.

    b.   60,000.

    c.   90,000.

    d.   135,000.

Exercises

1. Listed below are eight technical accounting terms emphasized in this chapter.

Fixed costs	*Contribution margin*
Activity base	*Relevant range*
Margin of safety	*Contribution margin ratio*
Break-even point	*High-low method*

   Each of the following statements may (or may not) describe one of these technical terms. In the space provided below each statement, indicate the accounting term described, or answer "None" if the statement does not correctly describe any of the terms.

   a. Operating income divided by the contribution margin.

   _____

   b. The amount by which total revenue exceeds total variable costs.

   _____

   c. Sales volume at which total revenue equals total costs and expenses.

   _____

   d. The percentage of each revenue dollar available to cover fixed costs and add to operating profit.

   _____

   e. The amount by which actual sales volume exceeds break-even sales volume.

   _____

   f. A method of dividing semivariable costs into fixed and variable elements.

   _____

   g. Costs that vary directly and proportionately with changes in the level of activity base.

   _____

2.   The information below relates to the Filtron Corporation:

Selling price per unit ....$ 26
Variable costs per unit...   20
Monthly fixed costs..$54,000
Maximum capacity per month (in units).............. 32,000

Complete the following statements:

a.   To break even, Filton Corporation must produce and sell _____ units per month.

b.   If Filtron sold 20,000 units, operating income would amount to $_____ per month.

c.   The maximum operating income that Filtron can expect to generate per month with its present capacity is $_____ per month.

d.   Assuming the cost of direct labor increased by $1 per unit, Filtron's maximum operating income would be $_____ per month.

3. Haley Corporation considers machine-hours to be the most appropriate activity base for manufacturing overhead costs. The following information pertains to the past four months of operations:

	Machine-Hours	Total Manufacturing Overhead Costs
January	5,000	$250,000
February	3,000	215,000
March	4,000	234,000
April	2,500	210,000

Apply the high-low method to complete the following:

a. The company's variable manufacturing overhead cost per machine-hour is $_____.

b. The company's fixed manufacturing overhead cost per month is $_____.

c. If the company planned to produce and sell 3,500 units in May, its estimated total manufacturing overhead cost per unit would be $_____.

4. Revcon sells three products: bats, baseballs, and baseball gloves. The contribution margin ratios of each product line are: bats, 40%, balls, 50%, and gloves 25%. Bats account for 30% of the company's total sales, balls, 10%, and gloves 60%. The company's fixed costs per month amount to $320,000.

a. Given Revcon's current sales mix, what is its average contribution margin ratio? Use the following table to compute your answer:

	Product CM Ratio		Percentage of Sales		Average CM
Bats	X		=		
Balls	X		=		
Gloves	X		=		

Average contribution margin ratio .... =========

b. What levels of sales must the company generate to break-even each month?

c. What level of sales must the company generate to achieve a before-tax operating income of $750,000?

d. Which product should management be thinking of ways to market more effectively? Explain your answer.

SOLUTIONS TO CHAPTER 20 SELF-TEST

True or False

1. **F** Cost-volume -profit analysis is a means of learning how costs and profits behave in response to changes in the level of business activity.

2. **F** Cost-volume-profit analysis may be used by managers to answer questions based on changes in levels of business activities. It cannot, however, replace the need for planning and budgeting activities.

3. **T** An activity base may be a measure of a key production input, such as direct labor hours. It may be a measure of output, such as units of production or units sold.

4. **T** A variable cost is one that changes in proportion to changes in the activity base. If no handmade goods were produced, the direct labor costs would be zero.

5. **F** Semivariable costs refer to costs that include both fixed and variable elements.

6. **T** Property taxes paid on a factory are considered fixed costs as they do not change in response to changes in the activity base. Property taxes remain the same regardless of how many units of output are produced.

7. **F** Direct costs, such as direct materials and direct labor, change in proportion to changes in the activity base. Thus, they are considered variable costs.

8. **F** Indirect costs may be fixed (such as rent on a factory) or variable (such as the glue used in a furniture factory).

9. **T** Variable costs rise and fall in response to changes in the activity base. An increase of 25% in the activity base would result in an approximate increase to total variable costs of 25%.

10. **F** The entire cost of operating a tractor would be considered a semivariable cost. The $3,000 refers to the fixed portion of the cost, while the 90 cents per mile refers to the variable portion of the cost.

11. **T** Unusual patterns of cost behavior are most likely to occur at extremely high or extremely low levels of volume. The relevant range is defined as the range over which volume is reasonably expected to vary. Thus, it would not include these two extremes.

12. **F** The contribution margin ratio is the contribution margin expressed as a percentage of sales. Item A may have a unit sales price much larger than that of item B, which would result in a lower contribution margin ratio for item A than for item B.

13. **F** The break-even point, on a cost-volume-profit graph occurs at the level of volume where total revenue equals total costs (both fixed and variable).

14. **F** The margin of safety refers to the amount by which actual sales volume exceeds the break-even sales volume. A business with a $100,000 margin of safety would incur an operating loss only if its sales volume declined by more than $100.000.

15. **T** The cost-volume-profit graph typically includes a total revenue line, a total cost line, and a total fixed cost line.

16. **T** The term "profit" in cost-volume-profit analysis generally refers to operating income rather than net income, as income taxes are neither a fixed nor a variable cost.

Completion Statements

1. Variable, fixed. 2. Activity base. 3. Mixed, fixed, variable. 4. Variable, fixed, $0.25. 5. Contribution margin. 6. Sales, fixed costs, operating income. 7. $3.00, 60%, $5.30, 53%. 8. X. 9. Sales, decrease, break even.

Multiple Choice

1. Answer **c**—the quantity chosen would be total unit sales. Total costs would be divided by units sold in order to arrive at the unit cost per item sold.

2. Answer **a**—as total fixed costs do not change significantly in response to changes in the activity base, dividing a fixed cost by a greater number of units produced would result in a lower average fixed cost per unit. Answers **b** and **d** (average semivariable cost per unit and average total cost per unit) would also decrease, but to a lesser extent because of their variable cost component.

3. Answer **b**—total variable costs rise and fall in approximate proportion to changes in the activity base, whereas variable costs per unit remain relatively constant.

4. Answer **b**—a 3,000-unit increase in production caused a $6,000 increase in cost. Therefore, the variable element may be stated as $2.00 per unit produced. Using the total monthly cost of $12,000 as the highest level, and deducting the variable portion of $8,000 (4,000 units x $2.00 per unit), we obtain a $4,000 value for the fixed portion (12,000 - $8,000 = $4,000).

5. Answer **d**—the break-even point occurs when a company is earning a zero profit. In other words, at a volume where total revenue equals total costs.

6. Answer **b**—*total* variable expenses in increase in proportion to increases in unit sales. However, variable expenses *per unit* remain constant within the relevant range.

7. Answer **b**—the break-even point is computed by dividing fixed costs by the unit contribution margin. Thus, a higher contribution margin would result in breaking even at a lower unit sales volume.

8. Answer **d**—sales volume in units can be computed by dividing the sum of the company's fixed costs and its operating income by its unit contribution margin of 80 cents. Thus, a sales volume of 135,000 units is required ($108,000 ÷ $0.80 per unit = 135,000 units).

Solutions to Exercises

1.

   a. None (Not a meaningful statistic.)
   b. Contribution margin
   c. Break-even point
   d. Contribution margin ratio
   e. Margin of safety
   f. High-low method
   g. None (This statement describes variable costs.)

2.

   a. 9,000 units ($54,000 ÷ $6 per unit)

   b. $66,000 ($520,000 - $400,000 - $54,000)

   c. $138,000 ($832,000 - $640,000 - $54,000)

   d. $106,000 ($832,000 - $672,000 - $54,000)

3.

   a. $16 [($250,000 - $210,000) ÷ (5,000 units – 2,500 units)]

   b. $170,000 [$250,000 – ($16 x 5,000 units)]

   c. $226,000 [$170,000 + ($16 x 3,500 units)]

   a.

	Product CM Ratio		Percentage of Sales	Average CM
Bats	40%	x	30%	12%
Balls	50%	x	10%	5%
Gloves	25%	x	60%	15%

   Average contribution margin ratio 32%

   b. $320,000 ÷ 32% = $1,000,000

   c. ($320,000 + $750,000) ÷ 32% = $3,343,750

   d. Management should concentrate its efforts on marketing baseballs more effectively because, on sales dollar basis, baseballs contribute the most (50%) to total profit.

Highlights of the Chapter

1.   Identifying the relevant considerations in a business decision requires logic, judgement, and an understanding of financial information. The only financial information relevant to a decision is that which *varies* among the alternative courses of action being considered. Costs or revenue which *do not vary* among alternative courses of action are *not relevant* to the decision.

2.   The additional costs that will be incurred by pursuing one course of action rather than another are called *incremental costs*. Likewise, the additional revenue earned by a specific course of action is called *incremental revenue*. The analysis of incremental costs and revenue enables managers to compare the relative profitability of alternative courses of action and decide which one to pursue. This approach to decision making is called *incremental analysis*.

3.   *Opportunity costs* may be defined *as benefits given up by selecting one alternative over another*. In other words, opportunity costs represent value of benefits *that could have been received* had another course of action been taken. For example, you decide to go to college instead of working at the local hardware store for $6 an hour, your decision to further your education has an opportunity cost associated with it of $6 an hour. Opportunity costs are not recorded in accounting records, but ignoring them when making decisions can be a costly mistake.

4.   *Sunk costs* are costs that have *already been incurred* by past actions. As the only costs relevant to a decision are those which vary among the alternative courses of action, sunk costs, are *not relevant* in incremental analysis because they *cannot be changed* regardless of what alternative course of action is selected.

5.   In contrast to sunk costs, *out-of-pocket costs* are those costs which have *not yet* been incurred and which *will vary* among alternative courses of action. Out-of-pocket costs are normally identified as relevant considerations to incremental analysis.

6.   Incremental analysis is a valuable tool for many kinds of business decisions. We have identified several common applications of incremental analysis, including decisions involving: (1) *special orders*, (2) *productions constraints*, (3) *making or buying components*, (4) *selling, scrapping, or rebuilding defective units*, and (5) *joint product decisions*.

7.   *Special order decisions* involve the comparison of the special order's sales price with its incremental cost. Factory overhead which would exist *whether or not* the special order is produced is not a relevant cost. In short, special order decisions require managers to compare only the *additional costs incurred* with the *additional revenue generated* with each special order. If none of the incremental costs of a special order are considered *fixed costs*, the analysis of whether to accept it is based on the increase in *contribution margin* it will generate.

8.   *Production constraint decisions* involve deciding which product to produce when faced with limited productive resources (materials, labor, machine-hours, etc.). One approach to this problem is to manufacture the product which *maximizes the contribution per unit of scarce resource*. In most cases, however, a company cannot, simply devote all of its resources to manufacturing a single product. Thus, managers must consider many other issues, such as product demand, in deciding which products to produce. In addition to understanding the contribution margin of its products, a company must also attempt to understand the complementary nature of its products. That is, does the sale of one product contribute to the sale of another? Products for which sales of one contribute to the sales of another are called *complementary products*.

9. *Make or buy decisions* involve deciding whether to make or buy a component part used in producing a product. The relevant costs in determining the cost of making the part are the incremental costs per unit of manufacturing the component. Fixed factory overhead, which will continue whether or not the part is made, should not be included in the decision. In addition to the costs associated with make or buy decisions, managers should also consider issues of product quality, production flexibility, and supplier reliability.

10. *Sell, scrap, or rebuild decisions* involve deciding what to do with defective products. Such products may have been processed improperly, damaged, or made with outdated components. In making the decision to sell, scrap, or rebuild the defective units, it is important to realize that the costs incurred to produce the defective units are *sunk costs*, and are therefore not relevant to the decision. Once again, important factors other than incremental costs and revenue must be considered, such as product quality and scheduling issues.

11. *Joint product decisions* involve products that are produced from a shared production process. When multiple products are produced with common materials and production activities, they are referred to as *joint products*. At a certain point during the production process (called the *split-off point*), separate and distinct joint products begin to emerge. Managers must decide which products to sell at the split-off point and which products to process further into other products. Such decisions involve an analysis of the incremental revenue to be earned from additional processing and the incremental processing costs to be incurred.

12. The goal in Chapter 21 is to emphasize the types of information relevant to particular business decisions. In each of the decisions we examine, we stress the importance of identifying both financial and nonfinancial considerations. Nonfinancial considerations include product quality concerns, legal issues, and ethical responsibilities.

TEST YOURSELF ON INCREMENTAL ANALYSIS

True or False

For each of the following statements, circle the T or the F to indicate whether the statement is true or false.

T F   1. The only costs relevant to business decisions are those costs that vary depending upon the course of action selected.

T F   2. The difference between the cost of two alternatives is called the *incremental cost*.

T F   3. The only considerations relevant to selecting among various courses of action are the incremental costs and revenue related to each alternative.

T F   4. Opportunity costs represent the costs incurred in order to take advantage of a business opportunity.

T F   5. Sunk costs are only relevant if they exceed the incremental out-of-pocket costs associated with a future course of action.

T F   6. Special orders are profitable only if the unit sales price exceeds the average unit cost of production.

T F   7. In general, when total output is limited by the scarcity of a particular resource, a company should consider manufacturing those products which maximize the contribution margin per unit of scarce resource.

T F   8. In deciding whether to rebuild a defective batch of product, the cost of additional labor is considered a variable sunk cost.

T F   9. Fixed manufacturing costs are relevant to make or buy decision only if, by deciding to purchase a component part from an outside supplier rather than continue making it, the fixed costs are eliminated.

T F   10. Bi-Lo Manufacturing Company recently incurred manufacturing costs of $25,000 in the production of a defective batch of products. In deciding whether to scrap or rebuild these units, the $25,000 is considered a relevant out-of-pocket cost.

T F   11. The split-off point is the point at which separate and distinct joint products emerge from common materials and a shared production process.

T F   12. Financial considerations are always more important than nonfinancial considerations in deciding among alternative courses of action.

Completion Statements

Fill in the necessary word to complete the following statements:

1. Differences in costs incurred and revenue earned under alternative courses of action are referred to as _____ costs and revenues.

2. A(an) _____ _____ is the benefit given up by selecting one course of action over another.

3. A(an) _____ _____ is a cost that has already been incurred by past actions. Such costs are not _____ in incremental analysis.

4. _____-___-_____ costs are those costs which have not yet been incurred and which may vary among alternative courses of action being considered.

5. When faced with a scarce resource, such as available machine-hours, managers often produce the product which contributes the greatest _____ _____ per unit of the scarce resource.

6. Anderson Manufacturing produces product X and product Y. If Anderson's customers buy either product X or product Y, but not both, X and Y are said to be _____ products.

7. Those products for which sales of one may contribute to the sales of another are said to be _____ products.

8. The term _____ _____ is used to describe products that share common materials and common production processes.

Multiple Choice

Choose the best answer for each of the following questions and enter the identifying letter in the space provided.

___ 1. Costs that change as a result of selecting one course of action over another are referred to as:
- a. Variable costs.
- b. Opportunity costs.
- c. Incremental costs.
- d. Sunk costs.

___ 2. Which of the following is *not* a relevant consideration in incremental analysis?
- a. Out-of-pocket costs.
- b. Incremental costs.
- c. Opportunity costs.
- d. Sunk costs.

___ 3. Which of the following would be considered a *nonfinancial* consideration in making a decision to sell, scrap, or rebuild a defective batch of product?
- a. The incremental revenue associated with each course of action.
- b. The costs incurred in producing the defective batch of products.
- c. The quality associated with the products should the company decide to rebuild them.
- d. The increase in the company's contribution margin under each course of action.

___ 4. The acceptance of a special order will improve net income whenever the revenue from the special order exceeds:
- a. The variable costs of producing the order.
- b. The marginal cost of producing one unit.
- c. The incremental cost of producing the order.
- d. The cash expenditure of producing the order.

___ 5. Westport Ironworks has 10 furnaces which do not meet newly enacted "clean air" statutes. The furnaces must either be modified or replaced. Which of the following is *least* relevant to the decision as to whether to modify or replace the furnaces?
- a. The price for which the furnaces can be sold in "as is" condition.
- b. The cost to modify the furnaces to meet the clean air statutes.
- c. The current book value of the furnaces.
- d. The cost of new furnaces that meet the clean air statutes.

_____ 6. The Mazor Company manufactures 10,000 air filters per year. Each filter normally sells for $8 and has a contribution margin of $3. A special order for 2,000 filters at a reduced selling price of $6 would:

    a.   Decrease operating income by $10,000.

    b.   Decrease operating income by $4,000.

    c.   Increase operating income by $2,000.

    d.   Increase operating income by $6,000.

_____ 7. Tech, Inc., started out selling educational software to college students. Now, however, the company earns a large portion of its revenue from developing new business software. Tech's output is constrained by a limited availability of programming hours. Which of the following is *not* relevant in deciding which line of software to develop?

    a.   The contribution margin per programming hour of each product line.

    b.   Commitments to numerous school systems to develop new educational software.

    c.   The principal stockholder's personal commitment to meeting the needs of the educational community.

    d.   None of the above. Each of these considerations is relevant to the decision.

_____ 8. Oswald Manufacturing manufactures two joint products from common materials and production processes: product A and product B. At the split-off point, product A can be sold for $5,000, and product B can be sold for $15,000. If product A is processed beyond the split-off point at an additional cost of $3,000, it can be sold for $7,000. If product B is processed beyond the split-off point at an additional cost of $6,000 it can be sold for $20,000. To maximize its profit, Oswald should:

    a.   Process both products beyond the split-off point.

    b.   Process only product A beyond the split-off point.

    c.   Process only product B beyond the split-off point.

    d.   Sell both products at the split-off point.

Exercises

1. Listed below are eight technical accounting terms emphasized in this chapter:

Incremental costs	*Sunk costs*
Opportunity costs	*Out-of-pocket costs*
Competing products	*Complementary products*
Joint products	*Split-off point*

Each of the following statements may (or may not) describe one of these technical terms. In the space provided below each statement, indicate the accounting term described, or answer "None" if the statement does not correctly describe any of the terms.

a.   Products that share common materials and common production processes.

_____

b.   The differences between the costs incurred by pursuing alternative courses of action.

        _____

c.   Products for which sales of one may contribute to the sales of another.

        _____

d.   Costs incurred in the past, which are irrelevant to decisions regarding future actions.

        _____

e.   Costs which have not yet been incurred and which may vary among alternative courses of action.

        _____

f.   The benefit given up by selecting one course of action over another.

        _____

g.   The point in the manufacturing sequence when separate and distinct products emerge from common materials and shared production processes.

        _____

2.   J. Company uses 10,000 switches in its products each year. Each switch currently costs J Company $12 per unit to produce, based on the following total costs:

Direct material..$ 16,000
Direct labor.. 25,000
Variable factor overhead 20,000
Fixed factory overhead.. 59,000
   Total costs $120,000

J Company finds that an outside supplier will provide switches at a price of $10 per unit. If J Company stops producing switches, all of the direct materials, direct labor, and variable factory overhead will be eliminated, as well $10,000 of the fixed factory overhead. Use incremental analysis to determine whether J Company should make or buy its switches.

	Make the Part	Buy the Part	Incremental Analysis
Manufacturing costs:			
Direct materials	$16,000	0	$16,000
Purchase price @ $10 per unit	_____	_____	_____
Totals	$_____	$_____	$_____
Conclusion:			

3.   Franklin Company manufacturers many products. Three of these products include: product A, product B, and product C. Selected information pertaining to each product line is shown below

Product	Unit Selling Price	Unit Variable Costs
A	$25	$15
B	40	10
C	75	39

Products A, B, and C use common machinery in the manufacturing process. A total of only 300 machine-hours are available for these three products for the upcoming month. Each unit of product A requires 2 machine-hours, each unit of product B requires 3 machines-hours, and each unit of product C requires 6 machine-hours. Demand for each product far exceeds the company's ability to produce.

a.   Which of these three products should Franklin produce if it wishes to maximize its income for the upcoming month?

b.   Assume that product A and product B are considered "complementary" products. How does this influence your answer in part **a?**

4.   Anderson Electric makes power surge protectors for personal computers. Although the company has the capacity to produce 100,000 units per month, its current sales volume requires that only 60,000 units be produced. At this level of output, monthly manufacturing costs average approximately $360 per month, or $6 per unit, computed as follows:

Variable costs ($2 per unit x 60,000 units) $120,000
Fixed costs   240,000
Total cost at 60,000 units $360,000
Average cost per unit ($360,000 ÷ 60,000 units) $ 6

Assume that Anderson received a special order from Computer Universe, a large retail computer outlet. Computer Universe offered Anderson $5 per unit, and will purchase 25,000 units per month. To avoid competition with Anderson's regular customers, Computers Universe has agreed not to sell these units in Anderson's current customer territory.

a.   What financial information is relevant to Anderson's decision of whether to accept this special order?

b.   If Anderson accepts this order, by how much will its pretax operating increase or decrease?

c.   What other issues, in addition to financial concerns, should Anderson take into consideration?

Solutions to Chapter 21 Self-Test

1. **T** Costs, revenue, or other facts which do not vary among alternative courses of action are not relevant to business decisions.

2. **T** The relevant factors in decision making are the differences between costs incurred and revenue earned under alternative courses of action. These differences are termed *incremental costs* and *revenue*.

3. **F** In additional to incremental costs and revenue, numerous *nonfinancial* considerations must also be taken into account in most business decisions. These considerations may include legal issues, environmental concerns, and ethical responsibilities.

4. **F** An opportunity cost is a benefit given up by selecting one course of action over another. Although such costs are not recorded in a company's accounting records, they are important to most business decisions.

5. **F** Sunk costs are those which have already been incurred and cannot be changed. Regardless of their amount, sunk costs are irrelevant to current business decisions.

6. **F** Special orders are profitable if the unit sales price exceeds the *incremental* cost of production.

7. **T** When faced with a scarce resource, such as direct labor hours, the production of those products with the greatest contribution margins will *not* necessarily result in the greatest profitability. Instead, a company should consider manufacturing those products with the greatest contribution margins *per unit of scarce resource*.

8. **F** The additional labor costs required to rebuild the defective units is considered a variable out-of-pocket cost.

9. **T** Costs that do not change as a result of selecting one alternative over another are not relevant to a make or buy decision. Thus, unless fixed manufacturing costs change as a result of purchasing the component from an outside supplier, they are not considered relevant

10. **F** The cost incurred in producing the defective batch of products is considered a *sunk cost* and is not relevant in deciding what to do with the defective units.

11. **T** The split-off point is the point at which separate and distinct *joint products* emerge from common materials and a shared production process. Management must decide which products to sell at the split-off point and which to process further into other products.

12. **F** Nonfinancial issues are often as important as, if not *more* important than, financial considerations in making business decisions. Nonfinancial concerns often become financial issues when they are ignored. For instance, ignoring environmental statutes could result in large fines, clean-up costs, and legal fees.

Completion Statements

1. Incremental. 2. Opportunity cost. 3. Sunk cost, relevant. 4. Out-of-pocket. 5. Contribution margin. 6. Competing. 7. Complementary. 8. Joint products.

Multiple Choice

1. Answer **c**—incremental costs change among courses of action. Not all, variable costs are considered incremental costs, and not all costs that change are considered opportunity costs. Sunk costs do not change as a result of selecting one course of action over another.

2. Answer **d**—sunk costs do not change as a result of selecting one course of action over another. Therefore, sunk costs are not relevant in incremental analysis.

3. Answer **c**—incremental costs, revenue, and contribution margin are all *financial*, considerations in making a decision to scrap, sell, or rebuild defective products. Quality issues, however, are nonfinancial considerations.

4. Answer **c**—the relevant factors in this decision are the incremental revenues to be earned and the incremental revenues to be earned and the incremental costs that will be incurred by accepting the special order.

5. Answer **c**—the book value of the existing furnaces is a sunk cost which does not vary among the courses of action under consideration. As this cost cannot be changed regardless of the action taken, it is not considered relevant.

6. Answer **c**—if the filters normally sell for $8 and have a contribution margin of $3, we may conclude that their variable cost is $5. Thus, a special order for 2,000 units at $6 per unit will increase operating income by $2,000 [2,000 units x ($6 - $5)].

7. Answer **d**—each of these considerations is relevant to the decision at hand. The basic purpose of the question is to illustrate that nonfinancial considerations may be relevant factors in business decisions. In many cases, these nonfinancial issues may coincide with the best long-run financial interests of the company.

8. Answer **d**—product A provides a $5,000 benefit if sold at the split-off point. It provides only a $4,000 benefit if processed beyond the split-off ($7,000 - $3,000). Product B provides a $15,000 benefit if sold at the split-off point. It provides only a $14,000 benefit if processed beyond the split-off point ($20,000 - $6,000)

Solutions to Exercises

1.

    a. Joint products

    b. Incremental costs

    c. Complementary products

    d. Sunk costs

    e. Out-of-pocket costs

    f. Opportunity costs

    g. Split-off point

	Make the Part	Buy the Part	Incremental Analysis
Manufacturing costs:			
Direct materials	$16,000	0	$16,000
Direct labor	25,000	0	25,000
Variable overhead	20,000	0	20,000
Fixed overhead	59,000	49,000	10,000
Purchase price @ $10 per unit	0	100,000	(100,000)
Totals	$120,000	$149,000	($29,000)

Conclusion: Continue to make the switches

3.

a. The company should manufacture product B because it has the highest contribution margin per machine-hour. The necessary computations are shown below:

Product	Unit Selling Price	Unit Variable Costs	Unit Contribution Margin	Machine-Hours Required per Unit	Contribution Machine per Machine-Hour
A	$25	$15	$10	2	$ 5
B	40	10	30	3	10
C	75	39	36	6	6

b. Complementary products are those for which sales of one may contribute to sales of another. Thus, if product A and B are complementary products, the company may not be in a position to produce only product B. Instead, it may be forced to produce a combination of both products.

4.

a. The only financial information to this decision is: (1) the variable costs per unit of $2, and (2) the special order selling price of $5 per unit. The fixed costs are assumed to remain $240,000 in total, regardless of Anderson's decision concerning the special order.

b. Anderson's pretax operating income will increase by $75,000 [($5 - $2) x 25,000 units]

c. In addition to financial concerns Anderson should consider the effect that filling the order might have on its regular customers. Obviously, it would not be wise to sell these units at $5 apiece if Computer Universe resells them within Anderson's current sales territory. Anderson should also consider how its regular customers might react if "word gets out" about this special order.

RESPONSIBILITY ACCOUNTING AND TRANSFER PRICING

Highlights of the Chapter

1. Most businesses are organized into a number of different subunits that perform different functions. Organizing in this manner enables managers and employees to specialize in specific types of business activity. Companies use many different names to describe their internal operating units, including divisions, department, branches, product lines, segments, and sales territories. In our discussion, we generally will use the term *responsibility center* to describe a subunit within a business organization for which a designated manager is responsible for directing various activities.

2. An income statement measures the overall performance of the entire business entity. Managers also need, however, information to measure the performance of each responsibility centers within the organization. Such information assists managers in: (1) *planning and allocating resources*, (2) *controlling operations*, and (3) *evaluating the performance of responsibility managers*.

3. Responsibility centers are usually classified as cost centers, profit centers or investment centers. A *cost center* is business subunit that incurs costs (or expenses) but does not directly generate revenue. Administrative departments such as accounting, finance, data processing, and human resources management are usually considered cost centers. *Profit centers* generate revenue *and* incur costs. Within a car dealership, for example, sales and service represent separate profit centers. Profit center managers have decision-making responsibility over the control of resources used to generate profits. Their primary objective is to generate the highest revenues at the lowest costs possible. As such, profit center managers are often evaluated on the basis of their unit's profitability. Some profit centers also qualify as investment centers. An *investment center* is a profit center for which management has decision-making responsibility for making capital investments related to the center's business activities. A large car dealership may own and manage multiple showrooms within a city. Each location is considered an investment center if showroom mangers have decision-making authority for profit related activities *and* capital investment activities. Evaluating the performance of an investment center is somewhat more complex than the evaluation of a cost centers and profit centers.

4. An accounting system designed to measure the performance of each subunit within a business is referred to as a *responsibility accounting system*. Measuring performance along the lines of managerial responsibility is the primary function of such a system. A responsibility accounting system holds managers accountable for the performance of the centers under their control. In addition, these systems provide top management with information useful in identifying strengths and weaknesses among units throughout the organization.

5. The key to a responsibility accounting system is the ability to measure separately the operating results of each responsibility center within the organization. These results can then be summarized in a series of *responsibility income statements*. In these statements, revenue is assigned first to the profit center responsible for earning that revenue. Assigning revenue to the proper department is relatively easy. Computerized cash registers, for example, automatically classify sales by their department of origin.

6. In assigning costs to a responsibility center, two concepts are generally applied: (a) costs are classified into the categories of *variable and fixed costs*, and (2) each center is charged with only those costs that are *directly traceable* to that center.

7. In a responsibility income statement, variable costs are those costs that change in approximate proportion to changes in the center's sales volume. Sales commissions, for example, would be a variable cost included in the responsibility income statement of an auto dealership's sales department. Selling prices and variable costs are used in the determination of a responsibility center's *contribution margin*. The contribution margin is an important figure used in cost-volume-profit analysis.

8. For a business to be profitable, its total contribution margin must exceed its total fixed costs. However fixed costs cannot always be easily traced to specific responsibility centers within an organization. Thus, a distinction is made between traceable fixed costs and common fixed costs. *Traceable fixed costs* can be traced directly to a specific responsibility center and could be eliminated if that center were closed. The depreciation of tools used in a car dealership's service department is an example of a traceable fixed cost. Traceable fixed costs are typically subtracted directly from total contribution margin in determining a unit's *responsibility margin*.

9. *Common fixed costs* jointly benefit several parts of the business. The level of these fixed costs usually would not change significantly even if one of the centers deriving benefits from these costs were discontinued. For instance, the property taxes incurred by a car dealership would not change significantly if the dealership discontinued a profit center specializing in windshield replacements. Thus, property taxes are usually considered common fixed costs. Service department costs (e.g., payroll, accounting, etc.) are also considered common fixed costs by arbitrary means (however, activity-based costing greatly increases the portion of a company's total costs that are traceable to specific responsibility centers). Many companies simply charge each profit center only with those costs that are directly traceable. In this chapter, we follow the latter approach because: (1) common fixed costs often would not change even if a business center were eliminated (2) common fixed costs are not under the direct control of a responsibility center's manager, and (3) allocation of common fixed costs may imply changes in profitability that are unrelated to a particular responsibility center's performance.

10. All costs (common costs included) are traceable to *some level* of responsibility within an organization. As we move up a responsibility reporting system to broader and broader areas of accountability, common costs at the lower levels of management become *traceable* costs as they fall under the control of top-level managers.

11. The contribution margin provides an excellent tool for evaluating the effects of short-run decisions on profitability. Such decisions typically do not involve changes in a company's fixed costs. Unlike short-run decisions, long-run decisions often have fixed cost implications. Thus, the *responsibility margin* is considered a more useful *long-run* measure of profitability than the contribution margin because it takes into consideration any changes in fixed costs traceable to a particular responsibility center. Examples of long-run decisions often include whether to expand current capacity, to add a new profit center, or to eliminate a profit center that is doing poorly.

12. In summary, when making short-run decisions that do not affect fixed costs, managers should attempt to generate the greatest *contribution margin* for the additional costs incurred. When making long-run decisions, however, managers must consider fixed cost implications. This requires a shift in focus to *responsibility margins* and *responsibility margin ratios*.

13. In evaluating the manager of a responsibility center, it is important to realize that some fixed costs traceable to that center are simply beyond the manager's immediate control. In response to this type of problem, some companies classify traceable fixed costs as being either *controllable fixed costs* or *committed fixed costs*. Controllable fixed costs are those under the manager's immediate control, such as salaries and advertising. Committed fixed costs are those that the manager cannot readily change, such as depreciation and property taxes. In the responsibility income statement, controllable fixed costs can be deducted from the contribution margin to arrive

at a subtotal called *performance margin*. Committed fixed costs then can be deducted from performance margin to determine the responsibility margin.

14. It is common for the profit centers of large organizations to sell some of their output to other parts of the business. When products (either goods or services) are transferred from one department to another, transfer prices play an important role in the evaluation of departmental performance. A *transfer price* is the dollar amount used in recording these interdepartmental transfers.

15. Profit centers often use *market value* as a transfer price to other units within the same organization. To transfer goods or services at *cost* would produce no profit and would reduce the profit center's contribution margin. Likewise, the company receiving the goods or services at cost would appear to be getting a real bargain. Setting transfer prices becomes much more complicated if parts of a business are located in different countries. If goods are shipped across international borders, the transfer price may be affected by taxes, duties, tariffs, international trade agreements, and different determinations of market values.

16. Transfer prices are normally not paid in cash; they are reflected only in the accounting records as goods and services flow from one responsibility center to another. Because the revenue earned by the center supplying the goods or services is off-set by the cost to the center receiving them, transfer prices have *no direct effect* on the company's *overall* net income.

17. In addition to financial measures, many nonfinancial considerations can also be used to evaluate a responsibility center's performance. Such considerations may include the tracing of customer returns, defective parts, employee sick days, employee turnover, cycle time, market share, etc.

18. The Financial Accounting Standards Board (FASB) requires large corporations to disclose certain "segment information" in the financial statements. These disclosures include net sales, operating income, and identifiable assets of major industries and geographic regions in which the company operates. The responsibility center information appearing in the financial statements is *far less detailed* than what is developed for use by managers.

19. In a merchandising company, the cost of goods sold is entirely a variable cost. In a manufacturing company, however, the cost of goods sold is based upon variable *and* fixed costs of production. The inclusion of both variable and fixed manufacturing costs in inventory cost determination is the conventional accounting practice of *full costing* or *absorption costing*.

20.* *Full costing* is the approach we have illustrated and explained in Chapters 16–20. This is the approach *required* by generally accepted accounting principles and also by the income tax code. However, an alternative approach called *variable costing* often provides information that is better suited for managerial decision making.

21* Under full costing, fixed manufacturing costs are assigned to ending inventories of work in process and finished goods. Thus, as inventory levels "build up," a portion of a company's fixed costs are deferred, or carried forward, instead of being immediately deducted from the current period's revenue. These costs are later "released" from inventory (deducted from revenue) as inventories are sold.

22* Under variable costing, the variable and fixed manufacturing costs are shown separately on the income statement. Thus, the income statement may be arranged in the contribution margin format to allow managers to perform cost-volume-profit analysis.

23.* When using variable costing, only *variable* manufacturing costs are treated as product costs. Fixed manufacturing costs under variable costing are treated as *period costs* and are deducted from revenue costing, *only variable manufacturing costs are included in inventory and cost of goods sold.*

---

* *Supplemental Topic.* "Variable Costing."

24.* During periods when inventory levels are *increasing*, full costing results in *higher* reported segment margins than does variable costing. This is due to the fact that, under full costing, a portion of a company's fixed costs are deferred as inventory levels rise. In periods marked by inventory *declines*, full costing results in lower segment margins as previously deferred fixed costs are released and become part of the cost of goods sold.

25.* Under full costing, fixed manufacturing costs are part of the total product cost. On a per unit basis, the *fixed costs vary inversely with the number of units produced*. Thus, under full costing, performance measures such as cost of goods sold and segment margin are *affected by the number of units produced* as well as by *the number of units sold*.

26.* Variable costs are not affected by the level of production. Therefore, under variable costing unit costs, cost of goods sold, and segment margins are not affected by the number of units produced. The fact that the level of production *does not distort* these measures is one of its major advantages over full costing. The other major benefit is that the variable costing income statement is arranged in a manner that facilitates cost-volume-profit analysis.

27.* Although variable costing is a valuable managerial tool, it is *not acceptable* for financial accounting or tax accounting purposes. The reason is that by treating fixed manufacturing costs as period costs rather than as product costs, variable costing tends to *understate* the cost of creating inventory. This, in turn, *understates the profitability of a growing business* which may be experiencing rapid growth in its inventories.

TEST YOURSELF ON RESONSIBILITY ACCOUNTING AND PERFORMANCE EVALUATION

True or False

For each of the following statements, circle the T or the F to indicate whether the statement is true or false.

T F 1. Generally accepted accounting principles require that responsibility income statements be prepared for each profit center, but not for each cost center.

T F 2. A Sears store is an investment center, the sporting goods department in the store is a profit center, and the store's accounts payable department is a cost center.

T F 3. A cost center within an organization that incurs the lowest monthly costs is the most efficient cost center.

T F 4. One purpose of a responsibly accounting system is to hold individuals accountable for the performance of the specific segments under their control.

T F 5. In a responsibility accounting system, revenue and expenses should initially be traced to the largest responsibility centers, and then systematically allocated to the small responsibility centers.

T F 6. Fixed costs that recur every month are referred to as common fixed costs.

T F 7. Traceable fixed costs probably could be eliminated if the segment to which they are traced were discontinued.

---

* *Supplemental Topic.* "Variable Costing."

T F 8. All fixed costs become traceable at some level of the organization.

T F 9. Responsibility margin is equal to a responsibility center's contribution margin minus is common fixed costs.

T F 10. The contribution margin is useful in evaluating the consequences of short-term decisions, while the responsibility margin is more relevant in evaluating the long-term profitability of a responsibility center.

T F 11. Taken by itself, a negative responsibility margin suggests that the operating income of a business would increase if the responsibility center with the negative margin were discontinued.

T F 12. The performance margin is intended to measure the effectiveness of a responsibility manager, whereas the responsibility margin is intended to measure the overall profitability of a responsibility center.

T F 13. The performance margin exceeds the responsibility margin by the amount of controllable fixed costs traceable to the responsibility center.

T F 14. In evaluating the performance of a responsibility center manager, the income of the responsibility center should be charged with a 'reasonable share" of common costs relating to the responsibility center's operations.

T F 15. Profit centers are likely to establish transfer prices based on cost rather than the market value of the goods or services transferred.

T F 16. * In the published income statement of a manufacturing company, the cost of goods sold figure is a semivariable cost.

T F 17. * Under variable costing, all manufacturing costs are treated as period costs rather than product costs.

T F 18. * Variable costing always results in a smaller cost of goods sold figure than does full costing.

T F 19. * Variable costing always results in a higher net income figure than does full costing.

T F 20. * When inventories are increasing, variable costing results in a lower net income than does full costing.

T F 21. * An advantage of variable costing is that unit costs, the cost of goods sold, and segment margin are not affected by short-term fluctuations in the level of production.

T F 22. * Variable costing is required by generally accepted accounting principles but is not allowable for the purpose of determining taxable income.

---

* *Supplemental Topic*, "Variable Costing."

Completion Statements

Fill in the necessary word to complete the following statements:

1.   A(an) _____ _____ is a responsibly center of a business that incurs expenses but does not directly generate any revenue. A(an)_____ _____ is a responsibility center that generates revenue and incurs expenses, but does not have an identifiable asset base.

2.   A(an) _____ accounting system measures separately the performance of each responsibility center that is under the direction of a particular manager.

3.   _____ fixed costs benefit only on responsibility center of a business and could be eliminated if that center were discontinued. _____ fixed costs, on the other hand, jointly benefit several responsibility centers of the business and might be unaffected by the discontinuance of one or more centers.

4.   Responsibility margin is computed by subtracting _____ fixed costs from a responsibility center's _____ _____.

5.   _____ margin is a useful toll for evaluating the probable effect of a responsibility center's short-run strategies on operating income. However, _____ margin is a more useful tool for identifying those segments with the greatest long-term profit potential.

6.   Cost centers typically establish transfer prices based on _____, whereas profit centers base their transfer prices on _____ _____.

7. *   Under full costing, fixed manufacturing costs are viewed as _____ costs. Under variable costing, these costs are viewed as _____ costs. The method required for use in published financial statements is _____ costing.

8. *   When inventories are increasing, _____ costing results in a higher segment margin than will _____ costing. When inventories are decreasing, variable costing will result in a (higher/lower) _____ segment margin than will full costing.

---

* *Supplemental Topic*, "Variable Costing."

Multiple Choice

Choose the best answer for each of the following questions and enter the identifying letter in the space provided.

___ 1.   A responsibility accounting system offers all of the following advantages to a business *except*:

      a.   Identify profitable and unprofitable responsibility centers of the business.

      b.   Hold managers accountable for the performance of their responsibility centers.

      c.   Reduce the number of accounts needed to record revenue and expense transactions.

      d.   Evaluate managerial performance against expectations set forth in departmental.

___ 2.   Contribution margin is *not* equal to:

      a.   A responsibility center's performance margin plus its controllable fixed costs.

      b.   The responsibility margin plus common fixed costs.

      c.   A responsibility center's revenue minus its variable costs.

      d.   A responsibility center's committed fixed costs, plus its responsibility margin, plus its controllable fixed costs.

___ 3.   Which of the following is a common fixed cost from the viewpoint of the Service Department in a Toyota dealership?

      a.   The cost of parts used in repairing automobiles.

      b.   The monthly salary paid to the manager of the Sales department.

      c.   Depreciation on tools and equipment used to repair automobiles.

      d.   Property taxes paid on the dealership's land and buildings.

___ 4.   If an additional $5,000 expenditure for advertising will cause a $20,000 increase in sales, the greatest benefit for the entire company will result by spending the money on the profit center with the highest:

      a.   Contribution margin ratio.

      b.   Performance margin.

      c.   Responsibility margin.

      d.   Rate of return on investment (responsibility margin divided by average identifiable assets.)

___ 5.   In which of the following decisions is responsibility margin more relevant than contribution margin or performance margin?

      a.   In deciding which product line will benefit most from an advertising campaign.

      b.   In deciding whether to cut a responsibility center's selling prices by 10% if this action is expected to increase sales by 25%.

      c.   In deciding whether to eliminate a particular profit center.

      d.   In evaluating the performance of a responsibility center manager.

___ 6.   Which of the following would a profit center **least likely** support for the goods it sells to other responsibility centers within the business?

    a.   Transferring the goods as their cost.

    b.   Transferring the goods as their market value.

    c.   Transferring the goods as their market value plus 10%.

    d.   Profit centers do not sell goods to other responsibility centers.

___ 7. *   Reasons for using variable costing include all of the following **except:**

    a.   Fluctuations in the number of units manufactured do not affect unit costs when variable costing is used.

    b.   Taxable income is reduced when variable costing is used, especially for a growing company with steadily increasing inventories.

    c.   The income statement can be arranged to show contribution margin as a subtotal when variable costing is used.

    d.   Costs can be classified in a manner that facilitates cost-volume-profit analysis when variable costing is used.

___ 8. *   Creative Games manufactured 20,000 chess sets for which it incurred fixed manufacturing costs of $60,000 and variable manufacturing costs of $7 per set. During the period, 15,000 of these chess sets were actually sold. Under variable costing, total manufacturing costs deducted from revenue for the period amounted to:

    a. $200,000.

    b. $165,000.

    c. $150,000.

    d. $ 95,000.

Exercises

1.   Listed below are eight technical accounting terms emphasized in this chapter.

Profit center	*Contribution margin*
Cost center	*Traceable fixed cost*
Investment center	*Common fixed cost*
Transfer price	*Responsibility Center*

Each of the following statements may (or may not) describe one of these technical terms. In the space provided below each statement, indicate the accounting term described, or answer "None" if the statement does not correctly describe any of the terms.

a.   The part of a business for which a particular manager is held responsible.

_____

---
* *Supplemental Topic*, "Variable Costing."

b. The amount charged by a responsibility center for the goods and services it sells to other center within the organization.

_____

c. A profit center for which management is able to objectively measure the cost of assets used in the center's operations.

_____

d. Sales minus total variable costs.

_____

e. A responsibility center such as an accounting department, advertising department, or human resources department.

_____

f. Costs that jointly benefit two or more responsibility centers of the same business.

_____

g. A cost that typically changes in proportion to fluctuations in sales volume.

_____

2. Complete the following responsibility income statement for Kumo Toy Co. Conclude the income statement with income from operations for the entire company. Fill in the missing captions, percentages, and dollar amounts.

KUMO TOY CO.
Income Statement Segmented by Product Lines
For the Current Month

| | Kumo Toy Co. | | Segments | | | |
| | | | Toys | | Games | |
	Dollars	%	Dollars	%	Dollars	%
Sales	$500,000	100	$300,000	100	$200,000	100
Variable costs	_____	___	_____	30	_____	40
			$		$	
Traceable fixed costs	$_____	39	135,000			
	60,000	___	$_____	___	$_____	___
Income from operations	$					
Income tax expense	25,000	___				
Net income	$_____	___				

93

3. The Electric Motor Division of MSB Corporation supplies the Air Conditioning Division motors used in its air conditioners. The company uses a cost-plus approach to establish a transfer price between its two divisions. The agreed upon mark-up over cost is 30%.

Complete the following table:

	Electric Motor Division	Air Conditioner Division	Total Company
Revenue per unit	$400	$1,000	
Cost per motor	$250	-	
Costs from Electric Motor Division	-		-
Other costs	-	$275	
Gross profit			
Return on sales			

*4. Phoenix Mfg. Co. manufactures a single product. During its first year of operations, variable manufacturing costs amounted to *$15 per unit,* and fixed manufacturing costs totaled *$900,000*. Compute the company's cost of goods sold for its first year of operations under each of the following assumptions.

a. Full costing was used, and 90,000 units were manufactured and sold. $_____

b. Variable costing was used, and 90,000 units were manufactured and sold. $_____

c. Full costing was used, 100,000 units were manufactured, and 90,000 units were sold. $_____

d. Variable costing was used, 100,000 units were manufactured, and 90,000 units were sold. $_____

Solutions to Chapter 22 Self-Test

1. **F** Responsibility center information is intended for use only by management and, therefore, is not governed by generally accepted accounting principles.

2. **T** The assets relating to the entire store can be readily identified, but the sporting goods department shares the use of many assets with other departments. The accounts payable department does not directly generate any revenue.

3. **F** The cost center incurring the lowest monthly cost is not necessarily the most efficient. Different cost centers perform different functions. In evaluating the efficiency of any given, cost center, it is necessary to consider the nature, quantity, and quality of the services it performs.

4. **T** A responsibility accounting system is organized to measure performance along the line of managerial responsibility.

---

* *Supplemental Topic*, "Variable Costing."

5. **F** Revenue and expenses should initially be recorded for the *smallest* responsibility centers. An income statement can then be prepared for the largest center by combining the revenue and expenses of the subunits within it.

6. **F** The term common fixed costs relates to costs that jointly benefit two or more segments of a business and, therefore, are not traceable to a specific segment.

7. **T** Traceable fixed costs relate to the operations of a particular responsibility center. Therefore, discontinuing the center should eliminate these costs.

8. **T** Costs viewed as common at the lower levels of responsibility become traceable to the larger responsibility centers. When an entity is viewed as a whole, all costs become traceable.

9. **F** The responsibility margin is equal to the contribution margin minus traceable fixed costs. Common fixed costs should not be assigned to individual responsibility centers.

10. **T** Short-run decisions usually affect only revenue and variable costs—the components of contribution margin. To be profitable of the long-run however, a segment must also cover its fixed costs. A company's ability to remain profitable over the long-run is often evaluated by the responsibility margin.

11. **T** If a responsibility center is discontinued, all of the income components of that center (revenue, variable costs, and traceable fixed costs) should disappear. Thus, if the responsibility margin had been negative, operating income for the entire company should increase. In practice, however, other factors should be considered, such as the effect that closing one responsibility center may have on the revenue of other responsibility centers.

12. **T** Responsibility margin measures the contribution of a responsibility center to the income of the entire business, yet may include costs that are not under the control of the center's managers. Performance margin is intended to measure the result of only those revenues and costs directly controlled by responsibility center managers.

13. **F** Both performance margin and responsibility margin are reduced by controllable fixed costs. Performance margin exceeds responsibility margin by committed fixed costs—which are those fixed costs not under the direct control of responsibility center managers.

14. **F** As common fixed costs are not controllable by individual responsibility center managers, they should not be considered in evaluating a managers performance.

15. **F** A profit center's performance would suffer if its transfer prices were based on cost. Thus, most profit centers establish transfer prices based on the *market value* of the goods or services transferred.

16.* **T** Full costing is used in published financial statements. Under full costing, both fixed and variable manufacturing costs are treated as product costs.

17.* **F** Under variable costing, fixed manufacturing costs are treated as period costs, whereas variable manufacturing costs are treated as product costs.

18.* **T** Variable manufacturing costs are included in the cost of goods sold under both variable and full costing. Only full costing, however, also includes fixed manufacturing in the cost of goods sold.

19.* **F** Variable costing only results in a higher net income than full costing *when inventories decreasing*. When inventories are increasing, full costing results in a higher net income than variable costing.

20.* **T** When inventories are increasing, full costing defers, as part of inventory, a portion of fixed manufacturing costs incurred during the period. Under variable costing, however, all fixed manufacturing costs incurred during the period are deducted from revenue generated during the

---

* *Supplemental Topic*, "Variable Costing."

period. Thus, when inventories are increasing, full costing charges a lesser amount of cost against revenue and thereby results in a higher reported net income. This condition reverses in periods that experience a decline in inventories.

21.* **T** Under full costing, fixed manufacturing costs are allocated to the number of units produced. Thus, fluctuations in production levels affect unit costs and, in turn, the cost of goods sold and segment margin. Under variable costing, however, all fixed manufacturing costs are deducted from revenue, as *period costs*, regardless of the number of units produced. Because variable costing bases unit costs solely on variable manufacturing costs, fluctuations in production levels do not influence unit costs, the cost of goods sold, or segment margin.

22.* **F** Variable costing is intended for use only by managers. *Full costing* is required by generally accepted accounting principles and also by income tax regulations.

Completion Statements

1. Cost center, profit center. 2. Responsibility. 3. Traceable, common. 4. Traceable, contribution margin. 5. Contribution, responsibility. 6. Cost, market value. 7.* Product, period, full. 8.* Full, variable, higher.

Multiple Choice

1. Answer **c**—A responsibility accounting system requires a very large chart of accounts, as revenue and expenses must be maintained for each responsibility center.

2. Answer **b**—To arrive at contribution margin starting from responsibility margin, we add back traceable fixed costs, not common fixed costs. Common fixed costs should not be charged to individual responsibility centers and, therefore, do not represent a deduction from contribution margin in arriving at responsibility margin.

3. Answer **d**—Property taxes on the dealership's land and building are common fixed costs because they jointly benefit all responsibility centers of the business.

4. Answer **a**—The contribution margin ratio indicates the percentage of a sales increase that is retained after covering variable costs. As fixed costs are not affected by this decision, the additional contribution margin to be earned should be compared to the cost of the advertising campaign.

5. Answer **c**—If a responsibility center is discontinued, all of its revenue, variable costs, and traceable fixed costs should be eliminated. These are the components of responsibility margin. Thus, if a responsibility center is discontinued, the operating income of the business as a whole should change by the responsibility margin eliminated.

6. Answer **a**—The cost approach is most likely to result in the lowest transfer price for the selling profit center. As such, it will result in the lowest performance measures for the profit center, as well. For this reason, the profit center's manager is likely to resist a transfer based on the cost of goods being transferred.

7.* Answer **b**—full costing is used in the determination of taxable income because variable costing is not acceptable for income tax purposes.

8.* Answer **b**—$60,000 + ($7 x 15,000 sets) = $165,000.

---

* *Supplemental Topic*, "Variable Costing."

Solutions to Exercises

1.

    a. Responsibility center

    b. Transfer price

    c. Investment center

    d. Contribution margin

    e. Cost center

    f. Common fixed costs

    g. None (This statement describes variable costs.)

2.

KUMO TOY CO.
Income Statement Segmented by Product Lines
For the Current Month

	Kumo Toy Co.		Toys		Games	
	Dollars	%	Dollars	%	Dollars	%
Sales	$500,000	100	$300,000	100	$200,000	100
Variable costs	170,000	34	90,000	30	80,000	40
Contribution margin	$330,000	66	$210,000	70	$120,000	60
Traceable fixed costs	195,000	39	135,000	45	60,000	30
Responsibility margins	$135,000	27	$ 75,000	25	60,000	30
Common fixed costs	60,000	12				
Income from operations	$ 75,000	15				
Income tax expense	25,000	5				
Net income	$ 50,000	10				

3.

	Electric Motor Division	Air Conditioner Division	Total Company
Revenue per unit	$400	$1,000	$1,000
Cost per motor	$250	-	$250
Costs from Electric Motor Division	-	$325	-
Other costs	-	$275	$275
Gross profit	$150	$400	$475
Return on sales	37.5%	40.0%	47.5%

Supporting computations:

Gross profit (Electric Motor Division): $400 - $250 = <u>$150</u>

Return on sales (Electric Motor Division): $150 ÷ $400 = <u>37.50%</u>

Costs from Electric Motor Division: $250 + ($250 x 30%) = <u>$325</u>

Gross profit (Air Conditioner Division): $1,000 - $325 - $275 = <u>$400</u>

Return on sales (Air Conditioner Division): $400 ÷ $1,000 = <u>40%</u>

Gross profit (total company): $1,000 - $250 - $275 = <u>$475</u>

Return on sales (total company): $475 ÷ $1,000 = <u>47.5%</u>

4.
a.	<u>$2,250,000</u>	90,000 units x [$15 + ($900,000 ÷ 90,000 units)]
b.	<u>$1,350,000</u>	90,000 units x $15
c.	<u>$2,160,000</u>	90,000 units x [$15 + ($900,000 ÷ 100,000 units)]
d.	<u>$1,350,500</u>	90,000 units x $15

HIGHLIGHTS OF THE CHAPTER

1. One of the most important facets of managing the daily operations of a business enterprise is making certain that cash *inflows* generated from operations adequately cover the enterprise's cash *outflow* obligations. Some companies, especially those experiencing rapid growth, experience *negative operating* cash flow, even though they are *profitable*.

2. Rapidly growing companies that are *profit rich, yet cash poor*, often have excessively long *operating cycles*. In other words, their rapid growth initially ties up significant amounts of cash in inventories and receivables. Meanwhile, cash obligations for payrolls, materials purchases, debt service and overhead items are all increasing in response to company growth.

3. The effective management of business operations demands that managers engage in planning and controlling activities. *Planning* refers to setting financial and operating goals of a business. *Controlling* refers to seeing that things go according to plan and that corrective action is taken when actual results fall short of plans—such as when cash outflows exceed planned cash inflows. *Operational budgeting* is a process to assist managers in planning and controlling business operations.

4. A budget is a comprehensive *financial plan* for future operations. The benefits of a thorough budget process include:

    a. *Enhanced managerial perspective.* Budgeting makes managers more aware of the economic environment in which a business operates.

    b. *Advance warning of problems*. Budgets often provide advance warning of problems such as cash shortages and rising costs.

    c. *Coordination of activities*. Preparation of a budget provides an opportunity to coordinate the activities of all departments within a business.

    d. *Performance evaluation*. Budgets provide a financial yardstick against which each department's performance can be measured.

5. There are two basic philosophies for setting budgetary "targets."

    a. A *behavioral* approach is widely used and involves setting budget targets at reasonably *achievable levels*—that is, at levels achievable through reasonably efficient operations. Budgeting under this approach often *motivates behavior* to "meet or beat" imposed budgetary requirements.

    b. A *total quality management* approach reflects the idea that every segment of a business must continually strive to improve. Under this approach, budgetary targets are often set at levels which demand *optimum efficiency*. As such, there is no room for a department to "beat the budget." Instead, any amount by which a department falls short of optimal performance indicates "room for improvement."

6. Selecting and using a budgeting approach reflects the philosophy and goals of top management. Regardless of the approach adopted, however, managers should be encouraged to *actively participate* in the budgeting process.

7. The period of time covered by a budget varies from company to company. However, *operational budgeting* (budgeting for the daily operations of a business) usually involves periods of less than one year (monthly or quarterly), whereas *capital budgeting* (budgeting capital expenditures for

plant and equipment) often covers periods as long as 5 to 10 years. Chapter 22 focuses on operational budgeting. Capital budgeting will be addressed in Chapter 24.

8. A *master budget* is a "package" of related budgets that collectively summarizes the planned activities of a business. The comprehensive nature of a master budget also enables managers to forecast and prepare *budgeted financial statements* for an organization. It also facilitates the preparation of budgets for the kinds of *responsibility centers* we discussed in Chapter 21.

9. The logical sequence for preparing a master budget requires managers to formulate numerous *operating budget estimates* and *financial budget estimates*.

10. *Operational budget estimates* refer to projections of a company's operating performance. As such, these estimates culminate in the preparation of a company's *budgeted income statement.* The specific projections include:

a. *The sales forecast*—projecting sales in terms of units and dollars.

b. *The production schedule*—determining the manufacturing requirements and the projected level of ending finished goods *stated in units*.

c. *Manufacturing cost estimates*—estimating variable per-unit manufacturing costs and fixed manufacturing costs for the budget period.

d. *Manufacturing cost budget*—forecasting *total manufacturing costs* for the budget period (both variable and fixed).

e. *Estimated ending finished goods inventory*—establishing a desired ending finished goods inventory *stated in dollars*.

f. *Cost of goods sold budget*—projecting cost of goods sold for the budget period.

g. *Budgeted income statement*—measuring anticipated operating performance for the budget period.

11. *Financial budget estimates* refer to projections of company's financing and *cash flow requirements* for the budget period. These estimates culminate in the preparation of a company's *cash budget* and *budgeted balance sheet*. The specific projections include:

a. *Budgeted direct materials purchases and inventory*—determining required direct materials purchases and establishing a desired ending direct materials inventory for the budget period.

b. *Means of financing costs and expenses*—identifying how budgeted costs and expenses for the budget period will be financed.

c. *Payments on current payables*—estimating required cash disbursements on current payables for the budget period.

d. *Prepayments budget*—determining prepayment requirements for the period and estimating ending prepayment balances.

e. *Debt service budget*—estimating required payments on outstanding debts at the end of the budget period.

f. *Budgeted income taxes*—determining quarterly income tax payments and the anticipated income tax liability outstanding at the end of the budget period.

g. *Estimated cash receipts from customers*—estimating cash collections on accounts receivable for the budget period.

h. *Budgeted accounts receivable*—estimating the ending accounts receivable balance at the end of the budget period.

i. *The cash budget*—estimating sources and uses of cash for the budget period and determining whether obligations can be met without additional financing.

j. *Budgeted balance sheets*—formulating the company's projected financial position at the end of the budget period.

12. Budgets alert managers in advance of potential threats and opportunities that a company may face in the future. Budgets also promote coordination among various segments of a business by getting individual managers to **communicate with each other**.

13. *A flexible budget is a series of budget projections for different levels of activity*. Use of a flexible budget prevents the budget from becoming "obsolete" should expected changes in a business activity occur.

14. Flexible budgeting may be viewed as a combination of the budgeting concepts and cost-volume-profit relationships. Thus, flexible budgeting is a valuable planning tool that allows managers to measure operating efficiency at any level of production within a company's relevant range.

15. Flexible budgets are often used for *performance evaluation purposes* to objectively measure the effectiveness of individual managers for a given level of output achieved during the period.

16. There are many software packages available to assist managers in budgeting activities. Many managers actually custom develop their own budgeting programs using spreadsheet and database applications.

TEST YOURSELF ON OPERATIONAL BUDGETING

True or False

For each of the following statements, circle the T or the F to indicate whether the statement is true or false.

T F   1. To be profitable, a company must have positive operating cash flows.

T F   2. Companies undergoing rapid growth must often deal with longer operating cycles.

T F   3. As inventory turnover and accounts receivable turnover decrease, a company's operating cycle becomes longer.

T F   4. Not-for-profit organizations, such as churches and hospitals, do not usually engage in budgeting.

T F   5. Budgets are used by managers to forecast a company's income, cash flow, and changes in financial position.

T F   6. A budget can be viewed as a fund from which expenditures are made.

T F   7. Virtually all budgets involve a forecast of future events.

T F   8. A behavioral approach to setting budgetary targets strives to achieve perfection by completely eliminating operating inefficiency.

T F   9. A master budget establishes a maximum level of spending which can not be exceeded.

T F   10. A responsibility budget may be viewed as a financial plan for use by segment managers.

T F   11. Capital expenditures budgets are usually long-term, whereas cash budgets are usually short term.

T F   12. Budgets are useful tools for planning, but have little to do with controlling a business enterprise.

T F   13. Forecasts of sales, units of production, and operating expenses are all necessary to prepare a master budget.

T F   14. The financial budget estimates necessary to prepare a master budget include a production schedule.

T F   15. The payment of a bank loan reduces assets and liabilities by the same amount and would therefore not appear on a cash budget.

T F   16. A flexible budget enables management to evaluate performance at *actual* levels of activity rather than at a predetermined level set during the budget process.

Completion Statements

Fill in the necessary word to complete the following statements:

1.   A rapidly growing company can become profit rich, yet cash poor, if its operating cycle increases to the point that an excessive amount of cash becomes tied up in _____ and _____ _____.

2.   A budget may be viewed as a _____ _____ that sets forth the expected route for achieving the financial and operational objectives of an organization.

3.   The _____ approach to setting budgetary targets is based on the premise that managers will remain motivated if they perceive the budget as being fair.

4.   The _____ _____ budget is a long-term plan summarizing investments in plant and equipment.

5.   A _____ _____ consists of a number of related budgets that collectively summarize the planned activities of a business.

6.   The portion of a budget relating to an individual responsibility center of a business is sometimes called a _____ budget.

7.   The first step in developing a master budget is the preparation of a _____ _____.

8.   The use of a budget serves the control function in two ways: (a) by identifying areas in need of _____ _____ and (b) by serving as a yardstick for evaluating _____ _____.

Multiple Choice

Choose the best answer for each of the following questions and enter the identifying letter in the space provided.

___ 1.   Which of the following is *not* a benefit derived from budgeting?

      a.   Management is made more aware of the economic environment of the business.

      b.   The budget may provide advance warning of future economic problems.

      c.   The budget fund provides assurance that cash will be available to meet budgeted expenditures.

      d.   The budget provides a yardstick for evaluation managerial performance.

___ 2.   Which of the following is a factor that causes a rapidly growing business to become profit rich, yet cash poor?

      a.   Slow sales growth.

      b.   An unusually short operating cycle.

      c.   Fast inventory turnover.

      d.   Slow accounts receivable turnover.

___ 3.   Which of the following is a characteristic of the total quality approach to setting budgetary targets?

      a.   Absolute efficiency.

      b.   A perception that the budget is fair.

      c.   Budgetary targets that are reasonable.

      d.   Budgeted performance expectations that can be exceeded.

___ 4.   Which of the following is an element of a master budget discussed in Chapter 22?

      a.   A labor efficiency budget.

      b.   A waste and spoilage budget.

      c.   A production schedule.

      d.   An employee turnover budget.

___ 5.   Which of the following is *not* considered an *operating* budget estimate?

      a.   A production schedule.

      b.   A manufacturing cost budget.

      c.   A cost of goods sold budget.

      d.   A direct materials purchases and inventory budget.

6. Which of the following is *not* considered a *financial* budget estimate?

    a.   A prepayments budget.

    b.   A debt service budget.

    c.   A budgeted income statement.

    d.   An income taxes budget.

7. Which of the following steps in the preparation of a master budget would logically be performed first?

    a.   Prepare a production schedule.

    b.   Prepare a sales forecast.

    c.   Prepare a cash budget.

    d.   Prepare a budget of manufacturing costs.

8. With respect to flexible budgeting, all of the following statements are true *except*:

    a.   One reason for preparing a flexible budget is that fixed costs vary dramatically at different levels of production.

    b.   Variance from budgeted amounts are more meaningful if the budget is adjusted to reflect actual levels of production.

    c.   Flexible budgets can be adjusted to show budgeted revenue, costs, and cash flows at different levels of activity.

    d.   The concepts of flexible budgeting are a combination of budgeting concepts and the concepts of cost-volume-profit analysis.

Exercises

1. Listed below are eight technical accounting terms emphasized in this chapter?

Continuous budgeting	*Financial budget estimates*
Master budget	*Operating budget estimates*
Flexible budget	*Responsibility budget*
Operating cycle	*Sales forecast*

Each of the following statements may (or may not) describe one of these technical terms. In the space provided below each statement, indicate the accounting term described, or answer "None" if the statement does not correctly describe any of the terms.

a. The starting point in the preparation of a master budget.

    _____

b. Estimates from which budgeted income from operations is derived.

    _____

c. The average time period between the purchase of direct materials and the conversion of these materials back into cash.

    _____

d.   Estimates from which cash budgets and budgeted balance sheets are derived.

_____

e.   Budget estimates of the planned production of finished goods and the desired level of ending finished goods inventory.

_____

f.   A set of related budgets that collectively summarize all of the planned activities of a business.

_____

g.   A portion of a company's budget that relates to a specific responsibility center of the business.

_____

2.   Use the following information to prepare Eagle Corporation's **December** cash budget.

  a. In November, 30-day credit sales totaled $120,000. Approximately 90% of these sales are expected to be collected in December.

  b. December sales are estimated at $200,000. Approximately 25% of these sales are expected to be collected in December.

  c. Total fixed expenses are budgeted at $30,000 per month. This figure includes $6,000 of depreciation expense. Variable expenses typically amount to 62% of total sales. All expenses requiring cash are paid in full when incurred.

  d. A $11,000 note payable plus $1,000 of accrued interest is due on December 31.

  e. On November 30, the company's cash balance is $18,000.

Eagle Corporation
Cash Budget
For the Month of December

Cash balance at beginning of month .... $
Receipts:

    Total cash available....................................... $
Disbursements:

    Total cash disbursements .... $
Cash balance at end of month .... $

3. The following flexible budget figures were prepared by the Salter Corporation:

	20,000 Units	30,000 Units
Sales	$160,000	$240,000
Cost of goods sold..	70,000	100,000
Gross profit on sales...	$ 90,000	$140,000
Operating expenses	25,000	35,000
Operating income	$ 65,000	$105,000
Income taxes..	26,000	42,000
Net income	$ 39,000	$ 63,000

Assume that the company's fixed manufacturing costs total $10,000, and that its fixed operating expenses total $5,000. Also assume that all variable expenses vary directly with sales and that the company's average tax rate is 40%.
Compute the following flexible budget estimates.

a. The company's sales at 40,000 units: $_____
b. The company's cost of goods sold at 40,000 units $_____
c. The company's gross profit at 40,000 units: $_____
d. The company's operating expenses at 40,000 units. $_____
e. The company's operating income at 40,000 units: $_____
f. The company's income taxes at 40,000 units: $_____
g. The company's net income at 40,000 units: $_____

SOLUTIONS TO CHAPTER 23 SELF-TEST

True or False

1. **F** Some companies can be profit rich, yet cash poor. A company can earn revenue in excess of the expenses it incurs and still experience negative operating cash flows.

2. **T** Companies undergoing rapid growth often experience increases in their inventory and accounts receivable levels. As inventories and receivables increase, cash becomes "tied up" for longer periods, resulting in a longer operating cycle.

3. **T** As inventory turnover and accounts receivable turnover decrease, cash becomes "tied up" for longer periods, resulting in a longer operating cycle.

4. **F** Planning for the future and controlling the use of financial resources is important for all types of organizations. Thus, it is important that all types of organizations engage in a formal budget process.

5. **T** Budgets are used by managers to prepare projected income statements, cash flow statements and balance sheets.

6. **F** A budget is a financial plan describing the expected path toward achieving organizational goals.

7. **T** The preparation of a budget is based primarily on estimates of future economic events.

8. **F** A behavioral approach to setting budgetary targets strives to improve efficiency by setting targets that are perceived as being *fair* and *reasonable*. Setting standards that completely eliminate operating inefficiencies would not, in most cases, be perceived as fair or reasonable.

9. **F** The master budget is essentially a "package" of related budgets which attempts to summarize the planned activities of a business. Planned operation, however, often differs from actual results achieved.

10. **T** A responsibility budget typically holds segment managers accountable for the results of their areas of responsibility.

11. **T** Capital expenditures budgets summarize plans for major investments in plant and equipment. Such investments often require many years of planning which necessitates the formulation of long-term projections. Cash budgets are typically prepared monthly or quarterly.

12. **F** Budgets are useful for both planning and controlling business activities. When properly developed, budgets provide advanced warning of potential problems, facilitate coordination among individual segments, and serve as yardsticks for evaluating managerial performance.

13. **T** The master budget is used by managers to prepare projected financial statements. Projected financial statements require forecasts of sales, production, operating expenses, and numerous other aspects of business activity.

14. **F** Although a production schedule is necessary in the preparation of a master budget, it is considered part of the *operating budget estimates*, not the *financial budget estimates*.

15. **F** A cash budget is concerned solely with the forecast of cash receipts and disbursements. The payment of a bank loan requires the disbursement of cash and would thus appear in the cash budget.

16. **T** The primary advantage of flexible budgeting is that is allows for the evaluation of performance at actual levels, even if such levels differ from budgeted levels.

Completion Statements

1. Inventories, accounts receivable. 2. Financial plan. 3. Behavioral. 4. Capital expenditures. 5. Master budget. 6. Responsibility. 7. Sales forecast (or budget). 8. (a) Corrective action, (b) managerial performance.

Multiple Choice

1. Answer **c**—a budget is a financial plan describing the expected path toward achieving organizational goals. Through use of a budget, managers become aware of cash flow requirements. However, the budget does not provide assurance that cash will be available as needed.

2. Answer **d**—a slow accounts receivable turnover can result in cash shortages as cash becomes "tied up" for excessive periods of time. Rapid sales growth, long operating cycles, and slow inventory turnover rates are also associated with a business becoming profit rich, yet cash poor.

3. Answer **a**—the total quality approach sets targets that require absolute efficiency to achieve. These targets can be perceived by managers as being unfair, unreasonable, and impossible to exceed.

4. Answer **c**—The production schedule was the only element of the master budget discussed in Chapter 22. Labor efficiency, employee turnover, and control over waste and spoilage are all important issues; however, they are not specific elements of a master budget.

5. Answer **d**—a direct materials purchases and inventory budget is a *financial budget estimate*, not an operating budget estimate.

6. Answer **c**—a budgeted income statement is part of the *operating budget estimates*, not the financial budget estimates.

7. Answer **b**—the sales forecast must be prepared first. Only when a level of anticipated sales has been established can estimates of production and operation expenses be formulated.

8. Answer **a**—budgeted variable manufacturing costs differ in total with levels of production. Budgeted fixed costs remain the same within the relevant range.

Solutions to Exercises

1.

    a.   Sales forecast

    b.   Operating budget estimates

    c.   Operating cycle

    d.   Financial budget estimates

    e.   None (This statement describes a production budget.)

    f.   Master budget

    g.   Responsibility budget.

2.

EAGLE CORPORATION
Cash Budget
For the Month of December

Cash balance at beginning of month		$ 18,000
Receipts:		
Collections on November credit sales		
($120,000 x 90%).......................................	$108,000	
Collections on December sales		
($200,000 x 25%).......................................	50,000	158,000
Total cash available......................................		$176,000
Disbursements:		
Fixed expenses		
($30,000 - $6,000).....................................	$ 24,000	
Variable expenses		
($200,000 x 62%).......................................	124,000	
Note payable plus interest	12,000	
Total cash disbursements		160,000
Cash balance at end of month		$ 16,000

3.

    a. $320,000 (40,000 units x $8 selling per unit)

    b. $130,000 ($10,000 fixed manufacturing costs + (40,000 units x $3 variable manufacturing costs per unit)]

    c. $190,000 ($320,000 - $130,000)

    d. $45,000 [$5,000 fixed operating expenses + (40,000 units x $1 variable operating expenses per unit)]

    e. $145,000 ($320,000 - $130,000 -$45,000)

    f. $58,000 ($145,000 x 40%)

    g. $87,000 ($145,000 - $58,000)

Highlights of the Chapter

1. Standard cost systems are used to evaluate and control various aspects of operating efficiency. In a standard cost system, *standards* are established for materials, labor, and overhead. Such standards are budgeted amounts that *should be* incurred to produce a product under *normal operating conditions*. Deviations from the standards, called *variances*, are investigated in order to determine if corrective action is necessary.

2. Standard costs are continually reviewed and periodically revised to reflect changes in the costs of materials, labor, and overhead. The manner in which standards are set varies among firms and industries. However, in nearly all circumstances, the process requires input from multiple perspectives throughout the organization.

3. *Direct materials standards* involve both the *cost* of materials and *quantity* of materials to be used. The setting of direct materials standards requires an understanding of related issues pertaining to cost, quality, and selling prices. The complexity of setting material cost standards often requires the expertise of purchasing agents, engineers, cost accountants, and marketing directors.

4. *Direct labor standards* involve both labor *wage rates* and the *time allowed* to produce a product under normal operating conditions. The setting of labor standards requires an understanding of issues pertaining to geographic location, industry trends, educational requirements, and unionization. Setting labor standards often requires the expertise of personnel managers, industrial engineers, union representatives, accountants, and factory employees.

5. Standard *overhead cost* per unit is based on an estimate of total overhead at the *normal* level of production. Standard overhead costs per unit are uniquely different than unit costs for labor and materials, because overhead costs are both fixed and variable. Activity-based costing may be used in developing standard overhead rates per unit. Once this standard has been established, overhead is applied to production at the standard cost per unit.

6. In a standard costing system, costs, are charged to Work in Process Inventory, Finished Goods Inventory, and to the Cost of Goods Sold account at *standard* amounts, not *actual* amounts. Any differences between standard and actual costs are recorded, in *cost variance* accounts. Favorable cost variances (when standard amounts exceed actual amounts) are recorded with *credits*, whereas unfavorable cost variances (when actual amounts exceed standard amounts) are recorded with *debits*.

7. Six *cost variances* are illustrated in Chapter 23: (a) the *materials price variance*, (b) the *materials quantity variance*, (c) the *labor rate variance*, (d) the *labor efficiency variance,* (e) the *overhead spending variance*, and (f) the *overhead volume variance*.

8. The *materials price variance* is the amount by which the standard cost of direct materials differs from the actual cost incurred. The variance is computed as follows:

MPV = Actual Quantity x (Standard Price −Actual Price)

A favorable materials price variance results from acquiring materials at cost *below* what has been established as the cost of materials per pound, per gallon, per case, etc. An unfavorable materials price variance results from acquiring materials at a cost *above* the standard costs.

9. The *material quantity variance* is the amount by which the standard quantity of direct materials *allowed for the number of units produced* differs from the actual quantity used. The variance is computed as follows:

MQV = Standard Price x (Standard Quantity – Actual Quantity)

A favorable materials quantity variance results from using *fewer* materials than allowed by the standard cost for the *actual* number of units produced during the period. An unfavorable materials quantity variance results from using *more* materials than allowed by the standard cost system for the actual number of units produced during the period.

10. The *labor rate variance* is the amount by which the average standard wage rate of direct labor differs from the actual rate incurred. The variance is computed as follows:

LRV = Actual Direct Labor Hours x (Standard Rate – Actual Rate)

A favorable labor rate variance results from the average hourly labor rate falls *below* what has been established by the standard cost system. An unfavorable labor rate variance results from the average labor rate per hour being *above* the standard rate.

11. The *labor efficiency variance* is the amount by which the standard direct labor hours *allowed for the number of units produced* differs from the actual direct labor hours worked during the period. The variance is computed as follows:

LEV = Standard Hourly Rate x (Standard Hours – Actual Hours)

A favorable labor efficiency variance results from using *fewer* labor hours than allowed by the standard cost system for the *actual* number of units produced during the period. An unfavorable labor efficiency variance results from using *more* labor hours than allowed by the standard cost system for the actual number of units produced during the period.

12. The *overhead spending variance* is the difference between the *standard overhead allowed for the number of units produced* and the actual overhead costs incurred during the period. The spending variance is typically the responsibility of the production manager. Costs that the production manager can control are referred to as *controllable costs*. Portions of the spending variance that are not within the production manager's control are referred to as *committed costs*. The overhead spending variance is computed as follows:

OSV = Standard Overhead Allowed – Actual Overhead Incurred

A favorable overhead spending variance results from actually spending *less* on overhead than the standard fixed and variable amounts allowed by the standard cost system for the actual number of units produced during the period. An unfavorable overhead spending variance results from actually spending *more* on overhead than the standard fixed and variable amounts allowed by the standard cost system for the actual number of units produced during the period.

13. The *overhead volume variance* represents the difference between manufacturing overhead *applied* to work in process and the *standard overhead allowed for the number of units produced*. The variance results from actual output differing from *normal* output levels. If actual output is *less* than normal output, an *unfavorable* volume variance results. If actual output is *more* than normal output, a *favorable* volume variance results. The overhead volume variance is computed as follows:

OVV = Manufacturing Overhead Applied – Standard Overhead Allowed

14. In a standard cost system, manufacturing costs are charged to the Work in Process Inventory account at *standard* amounts. Thus, the Finished Goods Inventory account and the Cost of Goods Sold account also reflect standard amounts. At the end of the year, balances remaining in the variance accounts are typically closed to the Cost of Goods Sold account. If the amounts remaining represent a *material dollar amount*, the variances should be apportioned among the Work in Process Inventory, Finished Goods Inventory, and the Cost of Goods Sold accounts.

15. Different managers within an organization will have different perspectives on how their performance should be evaluated given the variances observed. For instance, a *favorable* materials price variance traced to the purchasing agent may have caused an *unfavorable* materials usage variance for the production manager, if the low cost materials were of substandard quality.

16. JIT systems often reduce unfavorable standard cost variances. For instance, by shortening cycle times and improving manufacturing efficiencies, JIT systems can eliminate unfavorable labor efficiency variances and significantly improve unfavorable overhead spending variances.

TEST YOURSELF STANDARD COST SYSTEMS

True or False

For each of the following statements, circle the T or the F to indicate whether the statement is true or false.

T F   1. Standard costs are budgeted manufacturing costs that should be incurred under *normal* operating conditions.

T F   2. Once standard costs are established, it is important that they do not change from period to period.

T F   3. The direct materials price variance measures whether the standard quantity of materials allowed for a given level of output was purchased at more or less than the standard price.

T F   4. The materials quantity variance helps managers determine whether materials are being used efficiently.

T F   5. An unfavorable labor rate variance can result from incurring excessive overtime costs.

T F   6. An unfavorable labor efficiency variance may mean that the standard time allowed to produce at a given level of output is set too low.

T F   7. The overhead volume variance is often called the *controllable* variance as levels of output are controlled by production managers.

T F   8. If actual levels of production exceed normal levels during the period, the overhead spending variance has to be favorable.

T F   9. If cost variance accounts are not considered material in their dollar amounts, they are typically closed to the Work in Process Inventory account at the end of each year.

T F   10. Standard cost systems can warn managers of potential production inefficiencies before any problems arise.

T F   11. The materials price variance is computed by multiplying the standard quantity of materials allowed for a given level of output, by the difference between the actual price and the standard price of the materials purchased and used during the period.

T F   12. The materials quantity variance is computed by multiplying the standard price of materials purchased and used during the period by the difference between the standard quantity allowed at normal levels of output and the actual quantity of materials used during the period.

T F   13. A favorable overhead volume variance occurs when actual output during a given period is greater than normal levels of output.

T F   14. An unfavorable materials price variance is most likely the responsibility of the production manager.

T F   15. The complexities of implementing a JIT system often result in an unfavorable overhead spending variance.

Completion Statements

Fill in the necessary word to complete the following statements:

1. The _____ _____ variance focuses on the cost of direct materials purchases, whereas the _____ _____ variance focuses on the amount of direct materials used to produce at a given level of output.

2. The _____ _____ variance focuses on what workers were paid during the period, whereas the _____ _____ variance focuses on the amount of time taken by workers to produce at a given level of output.

3. The overhead _____ variance is typically under the direct control of the production manager. Those overhead costs that are not under the production manager's direct control are sometimes called _____ costs.

4. The _____ variance will always be favorable if the production level achieved during the period exceeds what is considered to be the _____ level of output.

5. In a standard cost system, cost variance accounts are usually closed to the _____ _____ _____ _____ account at year-end, unless their dollar amounts are considered to be material.

6. The materials price variance is usually the responsibility of the company's _____ _____, whereas the materials usage variance is normally the responsibility of the company's _____ _____.

7. Unlike unit costs for materials and overhead, overhead costs contain both _____ and _____ elements.

8. In a JIT system, long-term pricing agreements with suppliers can virtually eliminate an unfavorable _____ _____ variance.

Multiple Choice

Choose the best answer for each of the following questions and enter the identifying letter in the space provided.

___ 1.   Vangle Chemical Corporation manufactures a single produce called Zylax. Under normal operating conditions, 50,000 pounds of direct materials are purchased and used the production of Zylax each month, at a standard cost of $6 per pound. During the current month, the company purchased and used 40,000 pounds of direct materials at a total cost of $160,000. The company's direct materials price variance for the month was:

    a. $100,000 (favorable).

    b. $80,000 (favorable.)

    c. $80,000 (unfavorable).

    d. $20,000 (favorable.)

___ 2.   A favorable materials quantity variance is *not* likely to stem from:

    a. The use of experienced production workers.

    b. The use of high quality materials.

    c. Normal production levels exceeding actual production levels.

    d. A reduction in waste and spoilage of direct materials.

___ 3.   An unfavorable labor rate variance is *not* likely to stem from:

    a. Using highly paid employees to perform lower pay scale jobs.

    b. Poor scheduling.

    c. Excessive overtime costs.

    d. The use of high quality materials.

___ 4.   The most critical element of the total overhead variance is the:

    a. Volume variance.

    b. Committed cost variance.

    c. Spending variance.

    d. Fixed cost variance.

___ 5.   If actual levels of production for the period are less than normal levels:

    a. The overhead volume variance will be favorable and the cost of goods sold needs to be credited.

    b. The overhead volume variance will be favorable and cost of goods sold needs to be debited.

    c. The overhead volume variance will be unfavorable and cost of goods sold needs to be credited.

    d. The overhead volume variance will be unfavorable and cost of goods sold needs to be debited.

6. Which of the following is *not* true of a standard cost system?

    a. The Work in Process Inventory account is charged with standard costs.

    b. The Finished Goods Inventory account is charged with standard costs.

    c. The Cost of Goods Sold account is charged with standard costs.

    d. The cost variance accounts are charged with standard costs.

7. The materials usage variance is normally the responsibility of:

    a. The quality control manager.

    b. The production manager.

    c. The manager in charge of the purchasing department.

    d. The marketing manager.

8. Which of the following variances is most likely to be eliminated in a JIT system?

    a. The materials price variance.

    b. The materials usage variance.

    c. The labor rate variance.

    d. The overhead spending variance.

Exercises

1. Listed below are eight technical accounting terms emphasized in this chapter.

Standard costs	*Materials price variance*
Labor rate variance	*Materials usage variance*
Overhead volume variance	*Overapplied overhead*
Labor efficiency variance	*Overhead spending variance*

Each of the following statements may (or may not) describe one of these technical terms. In the space provided below each statement, indicate the accounting term described, or answer "None" if the statement does not correctly describe any of the terms.

a. The overhead variance sometimes referred to as the controllable variance.

_____

b. The variance that compares the labor hours allowed to produce at a given level of output with the actual hours required.

_____

c. Costs that must be removed from a standard cost system when the overhead volume variance is favorable.

_____

d.   The variance that results from actual output differing from normal output in a given period.

_____

e.   Budgeted amounts that should be incurred to produce a product under normal conditions.

_____

f.   Costs that must be added to a standard cost system when the overhead volume variance is unfavorable.

_____

g.   A variance that is typically under the control of a company's director of purchasing.

_____

2.   During the current month, the Whinfry Company charged $30,000 of direct materials, $40,000 of direct labor, and $90,000 of manufacturing overhead to work in process. The company uses a standard cost system and its month-end variances are as follows:

Materials price variance (unfavorable)..$3,000
Materials quantity variance (favorable) 500
Labor rate variance (unfavorable)... 2,000
Labor efficiency variance (unfavorable).. 2,500
Overhead spending variance (favorable).. 1,500
Overhead volume variance (favorable)... 1,200

The ending balance in the Work in Process Inventory account exceeds the beginning balance by $2,000. The total standard cost per unit is $10. Compute the following:

a.   The actual direct materials costs incurred during the month: $_____

b.   The actual direct labor costs incurred during the month: $_____

c.   The actual manufacturing overhead costs incurred during the month: $_____

d.   The number of units completed during the month: $_____

3. Lextron Corporation is a small producer if glue products. During March, the company produced 9,000 cases, each of which contained two gallons of glue. To achieve this level of production, Lextron purchased and used 18,800 gallons of direct material at a cost of $26,320. It also incurred direct labor costs of $81,000 for the 5,400 hours worked by its production personnel in March. Manufacturing overhead for the month totaled $25,800, of which $6,000 was considered fixed. Lextron's standard cost information for each case of glue is shown below:

Direct Material Standard Price	$1.50 per gallon
Standard Quantity Allowed Per Case	2.25 gallons
Direct Labor Standard Rate	$14 per hour
Standard Hours Allowed Per Case	0.50 direct labor hours
Fixed Overhead Budgeted	$5,000 per month
Variable Overhead Application Rate	$2.00 per case
Normal level of Production	10,000 cases per month

Compute each of the following variances (be certain to indicate whether each variance is favorable or unfavorable.)

a. Materials price variance:

b. Materials quantity variance:

c. Labor rate variance:

d. Labor rate variance:

e. Overhead spending variance:

f. Overhead volume variance:

SOLUTIONS TO CHAPTER 24 SELF-TEST

True or False

1. **T** Standard cost systems utilize predetermined (budgeted) costs for direct labor, direct materials, and manufacturing overhead. Each standard represents what should be incurred to produce under normal operating conditions.

2. **F** Standards costs should be continually reviewed and periodically revised to reflect changes in production methods or in the prices paid for material, labor, and overhead.

3. **F** The materials price variance measures whether the *actual quantity* of materials used was purchased at more or less than standard.

4. **T** The materials quantity variance compares the actual quantity of materials used with the standard quantity allowed for a given level of output. Thus, it is a measure of how efficiently materials are being used in producing finished goods.

5. **T** Workers are paid an overtime *premium* for the hours of overtime they work. The higher rate associated with the premium could result in an unfavorable labor rate variance should overtime hours become excessive.

6. **F** An unfavorable labor efficiency variance may mean that the standard time allowed to produce at a given level of output is set too *high.*

7. **F** The overhead *spending variance* is often referred to as the controllable variance.

8. **T** If actual levels of production exceed normal levels, the overhead *volume variance* has to be favorable.

9. **F** If cost variance accounts are not considered material in their dollar amounts, they are typically closed to the *Cost for Goods Sold* account at year-end.

10. **F** Although traditional standard cost systems are valuable control tools, they alert managers to problems after the fact, rather than before problems arise.

11. **F** The materials price variance is computed by multiplying the *actual* quantity of materials used during the period by the difference between the actual price and the standard price of the materials purchased and used during the period.

12. **F** The materials quantity variance is computed by multiplying the standard price of materials purchased and used during the period by the difference between the standard quantity allowed for the *actual* level of output achieved during the period and the actual quantity of materials used during the period.

13. **T** Fixed overhead costs are applied to production on the basis of normal output levels. If actual output exceeds normal levels, fixed overhead costs become *overapplied* and, consequently, need to be *removed* from the accounting system. The removal of overapplied costs increases income, which is viewed as favorable.

14. **F** An unfavorable materials price variance is most likely the responsibility of the manager in charge of purchasing materials, not the manager of production activities.

15. **F** Many companies find that the benefits associated with the implementation of a JIT system far outweigh the costs. One of the primary benefits of a JIT system is the *reduction* of overhead costs. Thus, JIT systems are more likely to result in an overhead spending variance that is *favorable* than one that is unfavorable.

Completion Statements

1. Materials price, materials quantity. 2. Labor rate, labor efficiency. 3. Spending, committed.

4. Overhead, volume, normal. 5. Cost of Goods Sold. 6. Purchasing manager (or purchasing agent), production manager. 7. Fixed, variable. 8. Materials price.

Multiple Choice

1. Answer **b** — the actual cost of direct materials purchased and used during the month was $4 per pound ($160,000 ÷ 40,000 pounds). Thus, the $80,000 favorable direct materials price is computed as follows: 40,000 pounds x ($6 –$4).

2. Answer **c** — the materials quantity variance is *not* directly influenced by the actual level of production achieved during the period. Experienced workers, high quality materials, and reduced waste all contribute to a favorable materials quantity variance.

3. Answer **d** — an unfavorable labor rate variance is *not* directly influenced by the use of high quality materials. Overpaid employees, poor scheduling, and excessive overtime all contribute to an unfavorable labor rate variance.

4. Answer **c** — the most critical element of the overhead variance is the spending variance, as it represents the portion of the total variance that managers can *control*. The volume variance is a function of productive output, which is often externally driven by demand for a company's products.

5. Answer **d** — if actual levels of production are less than normal, fixed manufacturing overhead will be underapplied with respect to the amount budgeted. As a consequence, additional overhead charged to the cost of goods sold. These additional costs reduce income and are therefore viewed as unfavorable.

6. Answer **d** — the amounts in the variance accounts represent the *difference* between actual costs incurred and standard manufacturing costs allowed. The Work in Process Inventory, the Finished Goods Inventory, and the Cost of Goods Sold accounts are all charged with standard costs in a standard cost system.

7. Answer **b** — The materials usage variance is normally the responsibility of the production manager, whereas the materials price variance is the responsibility of the manager in charge of the purchasing department.

8. Answer **a** — In a JIT system long-term pricing agreements with suppliers can virtually eliminate the materials price variance. The other variances listed may be reduced by a JIT system, but probably not eliminated.

Solution to Exercises

1.

    a. Overhead spending variance

    b. Labor efficiency variance

    c. Overapplied overhead

    d. Overhead volume variance.

    e. Standard costs

    f. None (This statement describes underapplied overhead).

    g. Materials price variance.

2.

    a. $32,500 ($30,000 + $3,000 – $500).

    b. $44,500 ($40,000 + $2,000 + $2,500)

    c. $87,300 ($90,000 – $1,500 – $1,200)

    d. 15,800 units [($160,000 – $2,000) ÷ $10]

3.

    a.   18,800 gallons x ($1.50 − $1.40*) = <u>$1,880 favorable</u>

        *$26,320 ÷ 18,800 gallons =$1.40 per gallon

    b. $1.50 per gallon x (20,250 gallons* − 18,800 gallons) = <u>$2,175 favorable</u>

        *9,000 cases x 2.25 gallons per case = 20,250 gallons

    c.   5,400 hours x ($14 − $15*) + <u>$5,400 unfavorable</u>

        *$81,000 ÷ 5,400 hours = $15 per hour

    d. $14 per hour x (4,500 hours* − 5,400 hours) = <u>$12,600 unfavorable</u>

        *9,000 cases x 0.50 hours per case = 4,500 hours

    e.   [$5,000 +(9,000 cases x $2 per case)] − $25,800 = <u>$2,800 unfavorable</u>

    f.   [($2 per case + $0.50 per case*) x 9,000 cases] = $22,500 applied

        [($9,000 cases x $2 per case) + $5,000] = $23,000 allowed

        $22,500 applied − $23,000 allowed = <u>$500 unfavorable</u>

        *$5,000 ÷ 10,000 cases = $0.50 per case.

REWARDING BUSINESS PERFORMANCE

HIGHLIGHTS OF THE CHAPTER

1. Organizations have objectives and goals that they try to achieve in their operations. This chapter focuses on motivating employees, customers, suppliers, and others to perform in such a manner as to achieve these objectives and goals.

2. Motivating others to perform requires an accounting system to help create and set goals and objectives through planning and budgetary processes. Accounting systems must also be capable of measuring progress toward these goals, providing timely feedback, and allocating rewards for goal achievement.

3. The *Dupont system* of performance measurement was developed in the early 1900's as a method of setting goals and measuring progress toward achieving objectives. Realizing that product line profits were an incomplete measure of performance, Dupont's management created a system in which performance measurement was based upon *return on investment* or *ROI*.

4. The Dupont system divided ROI into two component parts: (1) capital turnover, and (2) return on sales. *Capital turnover* (sales ÷ total investment) tells managers about how effectively invested capital is at generating sales dollars (i.e., dollars of sales generated for every dollar of invested capital). *Return on sales* (earnings ÷ sales) is a measure of how effectively sales are converted to earnings (i.e., dollars of earnings generated for every dollar of sales). Operating income, as opposed to net income, is used to compute return on sales.

5. Under the Dupont system, a business gains an understanding of the return on investment it generates. Capital turnover helps determine whether adequate levels of sales are being generated given the amount of capital that is invested. To improve capital turnover, management can take measures to increase sales levels, or to reduce the level of capital it has invested. Return on sales helps determine whether adequate levels of income are being earned, given the level of sales achieved. Again, to improve return on sales, management can take measures to increase sales levels, or to reduce expenses incurred in generating sales.

6. The primary reason for using any performance measurement, such as ROI, is to motivate employees to make decisions consistent with the goals and objectives of the organization. ROI motivates managers to earn the highest profits possible while using a minimum amount of invested capital. However, there are three common criticisms of ROI: (1) the short horizon problem, (2) failure to undertake profitable investments, and (3) certain measurement problems.

7. The short time horizon problem occurs because managers frequently move from one job to another. As such, ROI may encourage managers to take short-term, as opposed to long-term, perspectives. ROI's failure to undertake profitable investments results from managers rejecting certain projects with the potential to increase the firm's overall ROI. Assume that a company's overall ROI is currently 10%. Undertaking a project with the potential to generate a ROI of 12% would therefore increase the company's overall ROI. However, if the particular division considering this project currently has a ROI of 15%, undertaking the project would reduce the division's current ROI. Thus, the project may be rejected if the division manager's performance evaluation is based upon a divisional ROI measure. The third criticism of ROI is the inherent difficulty in measuring average invested capital and the actual operating earnings associated with that capital. Many organizational units share capital resources making the allocation of capital among various units somewhat arbitrary.

8.   In response to criticisms leveled at ROI, other performance measures have been created. Two common alternative measures are residual income (RI) and economic value added (EVA). *Residual income (RI)* is a measure of the amount by which operating earnings exceed a minimum acceptable return on average invested capital. Residual income helps to avoid the problem of managers being motivated to reject projects that would increase the company's overall ROI if these projects have the potential to decrease divisional ROI. A popular variation of residual income is *economic value added (EVA)*. EVA uses a more refined measure of invested capital which takes into account the average after-tax cost of long-term borrowing and the cost of equity capital.

9.   ROI, RI, and EVA all focus upon *financial outcomes* as opposed to certain input measures. The *balanced scorecard* is a system of performance measurement that links a company's strategy to specific goals and objectives and provides measures of assessment and reward incentives specific to these goals across the value chain. The balanced scorecard approach focuses upon: (1) the customer's perspective, (2) the business process perspective, (3) learning and growth perspectives, and (4) traditional financial perspectives.

10.   The *customer perspective* of the balanced scorecard provides a means for employers to consider their customers' needs and the markets in which their products sell. Customer retention, customer satisfaction, and product quality are important elements of the customer perspective.

11.   Just-in-time inventory and total quality management are both embodied in the *business processes perspective* of the balanced scorecard. The balanced scorecard focuses on both internal processes (e.g., cycle time, order filling efficiency, etc.) and external processes (e.g., steps taken to foster strong relationships with suppliers and distributers).

12.   The *learning and growth perspectives* of the balances scorecard recognize the importance of employee satisfaction, retention, and skills development. To this end, the balanced scorecard focuses on the people, information systems, and procedures in place to promote organizational learning and growth. The balanced scorecard approach also attempts to measure the reliability, accuracy, and consistency of the information provided by the organization's information systems. These elements are essential in measuring progress toward goal achievement.

13.   The *financial perspective* of the balanced scorecard helps to view the company through the eyes of creditors and shareholders. By so doing, managers are better able to consider the impact of strategic decisions on various financial measures used by external constituents to evaluate business performance (e.g., return on investment, return on sales, asset turnover, residual income, and other commonly used performance measures).

14.   Criticisms of the balanced scorecard include its difficulty in: (1) assessing the relative importance among the four perspective discussed above, (2) measuring, quantifying, and evaluating certain qualitative attributes, (3) achieving clarity and a sense of direction when using the diverse performance measures associated with the system, and (4) determining whether the benefits derived from using the balanced scorecard approach outweigh the cost of designing, implementing, and operating such a system.

15.   Incentive systems play an important role in motivating employees. The most common form of management compensation is a fixed salary. In addition to a fixed salary, many companies also have implemented bonus systems for managers across all levels of the organization. Profit-sharing and stock options are two common approaches to bonus incentive plans.

16.   Important issues to consider when designing an incentive plan include: (1) time horizon of the plan, (2) choice of fixed versus variable plans, (3) use of stock performance measures versus accounting-based performance measures, (4) deciding between local versus company-wide incentive systems, and (5) choice of cooperative versus competitive incentive schemes.

TEST YOURSELF ON REWARDING BUSINESS PERFORMANCE

True or False

For each of the following statements, circle the T or the F to indicate whether the statement is true or false.

T   F   1.   The DuPont system is a relatively new approach to performance measurement based upon a firm's return on investment (ROI).

T   F   2.   The DuPont system helps managers to better understand the component parts of a firm's ROI.

T   F   3.   Return on sales is computed by dividing a firm's sales by its operating income.

T   F   4.   Capital turnover is computed by dividing a firm's sales by its total capital investment.

T   F   5.   A primary criticism of ROI as a performance measurement is that it often encourages managers to take a short-term planning perspective as opposed to a long-term perspective.

T   F   6.   Residual income (RI) is the amount by which ROI exceeds an acceptable return on average invested capital.

T   F   7.   Economic value added (EVA) is basically a refined measure of residual income.

T   F   8.   The balanced scorecard is similar to the DuPont system in that it focuses upon a single performance measure from a financial perspective.

T   F   9.   Employee turnover statistics are an example of financial performance measures in a balanced scorecard system.

T   F   10. The balanced scorecard is often criticized due to inherent difficulties in designing, implementing, and using it.

T   F   11. Nearly all companies pay fixed salaries to their management employees as part of their total compensation package.

T   F   12. Most bonus plans base the computation of a manager's bonus on the company's stock performance.

T   F   13. Fixed bonus plans work well in conjunction in complex compensation schemes such as a balanced scorecard system.

T   F   14. Incentive plans are often designed to allow teams of employees to share equally in performance outcomes, regardless of each individual's actual contribution to that outcome.

Completion Statements

Fill in the necessary word to complete each of the following statements:

1.   The _____ _____ of performance measurement was created in the 1900's and is based upon a firm's return on investment.

2.   The component parts of ROI in the DuPont system are _____ _____ and _____ ____ _____.

3.   The _____ _____ is a system of performance measurement that links a company's strategy to specific goals and integrates objectives across four business perspectives to achieve its strategic goals.

4.   _____ _____ _____ is a specific type of residual income that is computed using a firm's weighted-average cost of capital.

5.   The _____ _____ is a set of activities necessary to create and distribute a desirable product or service to a customer.

6.   _____ _____ are rights to purchase shares of a company's stock at a specified price within a specified period of time.

7.   A company's _____ ____ _____ is computed by dividing its operating income by its net sales.

8.   _____ _____ is the amount by which operating income exceeds a minimum acceptable return on the average invested capital.

9.   _____ _____ is a measure created by dividing sales by the average invested capital required to generate those sales.

10.   A _____ compensation system is designed to allow teams of employees to share equally in performance outcomes, regardless of each individual's actual contribution to that outcome.

Multiple Choice

Choose the best answer for each of the following questions and enter the identifying letter in the space provided.

___ 1.   The components of ROI under the DuPont system are:
   a.   Return on assets and return on sales.

   b.   Return on sales and return on capital

   c.   Return on assets and return on capital

   d.   Capital turnover and return on sales.

2. A company generated sales of $1 million and reported earnings of $200,000. If its investment in capital totaled $4 million, its capital turnover was:

    a. 25%

    b. 20%

    c. 5%

    d. None of the above.

3. A company with an average capital investment of $8 million reported earnings of $100,000. If its return on sales was 20%, what level of sales did it generate?

    a. $ 200,000

    b. $ 400,000

    c. $ 500,000

    d. $ 1,600,000

4. Which of the following is *not* typically a criticism of ROI?

    a. It may encourage decisions that are not in the best interest of the company as a whole.

    b. It may encourage too much of a long-term perspective, as opposed to focusing on important short-term issues.

    c. It may encourage managers to reject certain profitable investments.

    d. It is often difficult to measure a company's invested capital and operating earnings associated with that capital.

5. A company reported operating income of $2 million. If it had an average capital investment of $12 million, and a minimum acceptable return on capital investments of 15%, what was its residual income (RI)?

    a. $ 200,000

    b. $ 1,800,000

    c. $ 300,000

    d. None of the above

6. Which of the following accounts is *not* a performance measurement perspective in a balanced scorecard system?

    a. Financial perspective

    b. Customer perspective

    c. Business process perspective

    d. Return on investment perspective

7. Which of the following measures is *not* considered a financial perspective in a balanced scorecard system?

    a. ROI

    b. EVA

    c. Cycle time

    d. Bond ratings

8. An incentive plan that motivates individual employees to perform better than their coworkers is often referred to as:

    a. An accounting-based performance plan.

    b. A variable compensation plan.

    c. A company-wide performance plan.

    d. A competitive incentive plan.

Exercises

1. Listed below are eight technical accounting terms emphasized in this chapter.

Balanced scorecard	*DuPont system of performance measurement*
Stock options	*Return on sales*
Value chain	*Capital turnover*
Residual income	*Economic value added*

Each of the following statements may (or may not) describe one of these technical terms. In the space provided below each statement, indicate the accounting term described, or answer "None" if the statement does not correctly describe any of the terms.

a. A system of performance measurement that integrates performance with a company's strategic goals.

_____

b. A performance measure computed by dividing sales by average invested capital required to generate those sales.

_____

c. A system of performance measurement that examines the individual components of return on investment.

_____

d. A performance measure computed by dividing operating income by the average invested capital associated with the generation of that income.

_____

e. A performance measure computed using a firm's after-tax weighted average cost of capital.

_____

f.   The set of activities necessary to create or distribute a desirable product or service to a customer.

_____

g.   The right to purchase a specified number of shares of a particular stock at a specified price within a certain future time period.

_____

2.   Westlock Corporation operates two divisions: Division A and Division B. Recent information pertaining to the performance of each division is shown below:

	Division A	Division B
Average capital investment	$800,000	$600,000
Sales	500,000	300,000
Operating income	72,000	60,000

a.   Compute the ROI of each division using the DuPont system.

b.   Compute the residual income of each division assuming that the company requires a minimum return of 8% on invested capital.

c.   Assume that each division has an investment opportunity that is likely to generate a 9.5% return. Discuss how the use of ROI versus RI as performance measures might influence each division manager's decision to make this investment.

3.   The balanced scorecard looks at performance from the following four perspectives:
- Financial perspective
- Customer perspective
- Business process perspective
- Learning and growth perspective

Listed below are several performance measures often used in a balanced scorecard system.
Indicate which of the four perspectives is associated with each measure:

a.   ROI: _____

b.   Employee turnover: _____

c.   Sales returns: _____

d.   Cycle time: _____

e.   Bond ratings: _____

f.   Machine downtime: _____

g.   Market share: _____

SOLUTIONS TO CHAPTER 25 SELF-TEST

True or False

1. **F**   While the DuPont system is a performance measure based upon a firm's ROI, it is hardly new. The system was created in the early 1900's.
2. **T**   The DuPont system breaks ROI into two component parts: (1) capital turnover, and (2) return on sales.
3. **F**   Return on sales is computed by dividing operating income by sales.
4. **T**   Capital turnover is a measure of a firm's ability to generate sales from a fixed level of invested capital. It is most often computed by dividing sales by total capital investment.
5. **T**   As managers more and more frequently move from one job to another, ROI has been criticized for encouraging a short-term planning orientations.
6. **F**   Residual income is the amount by which operating earnings exceed a minimum acceptable return on invested capital.
7. **T**   Economic value added is a refinement of RI that uses the weighted-average cost of capital as an acceptable minimum return.
8. **F**   The balanced scorecard looks at performance from four perspectives, of which only one focuses on traditional financial measures.
9. **F**   Employee turnover statistics are examples of learning and growth measures in a balanced scorecard system.
10. **T**   The balanced scorecard is often criticized because of difficulties in designing, implementing, and using it in practice. Organizations can avoid some of these difficulties by limiting the number of measures used in each of the four perspectives that the balanced scorecard emcompasses.
11. **T**   Most managers receive a fixed salary component as part of their total compensation. Some have an opportunity to earn more through overtime pay and bonus plans.
12. **F**   Most bonuses are based on internal accounting information, not stock performance.
13. **F**   A fixed bonus arrangement does usually not work well in a complex compensation scheme like a balanced scorecard system.
14. **T**   Incentive plans designed to allow teams of employees to share equally in performance outcomes are commonly referred to as cooperative compensation plans.

Completion Statements

1. DuPont system. 2. capital turnover, return on sales. 3. balanced scorecard.
4. Economic value added. 5. value chain. 6. Stock options.   7. return on sales.
8. Residual income. 9. Capital turnover. 10. cooperative.

Multiple Choice

1. Answer **d** – ROI is a function of capital turnover (sales ÷ total investment) and return on sales (earnings ÷ sales).
2. Answer **a** – $1 million ÷ $4 million = 25%.
3. Answer **c** – $100,000 ÷ 20% = $500,000.
4. Answer **b** – Managers frequently move from one job to another. As a result, ROI may discourage a manager's willingness to make decisions based on long-term planning perspectives.
5. Answer **a** – $2 million – ($12 million x 15%) = $200,000.

6. Answer **d** – The four perspectives of the balanced scorecard are the: (1) financial

perspective, (2) customer perspective, (3) business process perspective, and (4) learning and growth perspective.

7.   Answer **c** – Cycle time is considered a business process measure to improve the quality of the manufacturing process.

8.   Answer **d** – A competitive incentive plan rewards individual performance and, therefore, motivates employees to do better jobs than their coworkers. This is in contrast to a cooperative incentive plan wherein teams of employees share equally in performance outcomes, regardless of each individual's actual contribution to that outcome.

Solutions to Exercises

1.
   a. Balanced scorecard
   b. Capital turnover
   c. DuPont system of performance measurement
   d. None (The statement describes return on investment).
   e. Economic value added
   f. Value chain
   g. Stock options

2.   a.

	Division A	Division B
Capital turnover	62.5%	50.0%
x Return on sales	14.4%	20.0%
ROI	9.00%	10.00%

   b.

Residual income	Division A	Division B
$72,000 - (8% x $800,000)	$8,000	
$60,000 - (8% x $600,000)		$12,000

   c. If ROI is used as a performance measure, the division manager of Division A is likely to invest in an opportunity expected to generate a 9.5% return. The manager of Division B, however, is likely to reject the investment opportunity, even though the company, as a whole, requires a minimum return on capital of only 8%.

   If RI is used as a performance measure, both division managers are likely to invest in an opportunity that is expected to generate a 9.5% return.

3.
a.	ROI:	Financial perspective
b.	Employee turnover:	Learning and growth perspective
c.	Sales returns:	Customer perspective
d.	Cycle time:	Business process perspective
e.	Bond ratings:	Financial perspective
f.	Machine downtime:	Business process perspective
g.	Market share:	Customer perspective

HIGHLIGHTS OF THE CHAPTER

1.   *Capital investments* generally refer to large expenditures made by a company to acquire plant assets. Managers must systematically prioritize capital investment alternatives to decide which proposals to approve and which ones to reject. The process of evaluating capital investment proposals and deciding how to invest a company's financial resources is called *capital budgeting*.

2.   *Capital budgeting* decisions are important because they involve large amounts of money committed for long periods of time. Once a capital investment has been made, it is often difficult or impossible to reverse. Thus, investment decisions should be based upon a thorough analysis of financial and nonfinancial considerations.

3.   Capital budgeting relies heavily upon *estimates of future operating results*. Perhaps the most important component of these estimates is the investment's potential impact on future cash flows. Because cash flow projections, and other financial estimates, involve a considerable degree of uncertainty, all forecasts must be carefully scrutinized to control the risk associated with errors in judgement.

4.   Many capital investments may not have objectively measurable cash flows. For these proposals, nonfinancial considerations often become deciding factors. Examples of nonfinancial issues may include ethical responsibilities, legal requirements, improved employee morale, scheduling flexibility, enhanced product quality, etc.

5.   There are many sophisticated techniques for evaluating capital budgeting decisions. In Chapter 25, we examine three common approaches: (1) *payback period*, (2) *return on average investment*, and (3) *discounted cash flow analysis*. The application of these techniques involves financial measurements and estimates. However, the interpretations of the results requires an analysis of important nonfinancial considerations as well.

6.   The *payback period* is the length of time necessary to recover the entire cost of an investment from its resulting annual net cash flows. When annual cash flows are uniform, the payback period is computed by dividing the amount of the investment by its annual cash flow. Short payback periods reduce the risk of loss associated with changing economic conditions.

7.   There are two major shortcomings of the payback period: (1) it ignores the total life of an investment and, therefore, its total profitability, and (2) it ignores the *timing* of cash flows and, therefore, the fact that the value of a future cash flow today is *less* than the actual amount to be received in the future.

8.   The *return on average investment* is the average annual net income from an investment expressed as a percentage of the average amount invested. The *average amount invested* is one-half the *sum* of the original cost of the investment plus its estimated salvage value. Alternative investment opportunities may be ranked according to their respective returns. Return on average investment considers the profitability of an investment, but ignores the *timing* of future cash flows.

9.   *Discounting future cash flows* is the process of determining the *present value* of an investment's future net cash flows. This technique considers both the *amount and timing* of an investment's future cash flows.

10.   The present value of an investment is the amount that a knowledgeable investor would pay today for the right to receive a specified future amount. The present value of a cash flow is always *less*

than the actual future amount to be received. This is because money on hand today can be invested to become equivalent to a larger amount in the future.

11. The present value of a future cash flow depends upon (a) the amount of the future cash flow, (b) the length of time until the future cash flow will occur, and (c) the rate of return (*discount rate*) required by the investor.

12. *A table of present values* shows the present value of *$1 to be received at various times in the future*, discounted at a various required rates of return. To find the present value of a larger amount, the present value of $1 is simply multiplied by the amount under consideration.

13. An *annuity table* shows the present value of *$1 to be received periodically* for a given number of periods, discounted at various discount rates. An annuity table can only be used to find the present value of a series of *uniform* cash flows. A table of present values and an annuity table are illustrated in your text. You should become familiar with their use.

14. The *net present value* of a proposal is the difference between the total present value of its future net cash flows and the initial cost of the investment.

15. A *positive* net present value means that an investment's rate for return is expected to be *higher than the discount rate*. Conversely, a negative net present value means that the investment's rate of return is expected to be *less than the discount rate*. In financial terms, investments with the highest net present values are often considered the most desirable.

TEST YOURSELF ON CAPITAL BUDGETING

True or False

For each of the following statements, circle the T or the F to indicate whether the statement is true or false.

T F 1. Well planned capital investments are usually easy to reverse should future economic conditions unexpectedly change.

T F 2. Capital budgeting decisions involve both financial and nonfinancial considerations.

T F 3. The average cost of an investment equals one-half of the original cost of an investment divided by the investment's estimated useful life.

T F 4. The payback period is the length of time required to recover the entire cost of an investment divided by the investment's estimated useful life.

T F 5. An investment with a short payback period is not necessarily a profitable investment.

T F 6. The return on average investment method of evaluating proposals takes into consideration both the amount and timing of future cash flows.

T F 7. The present value of a future cash flow is always less than its future amount.

T F 8. The present value of a sum of money to be received 7 years from now is more than the present value of the same amount to be received 10 years from now.

T F   9. Discounting of future cash flows takes into consideration both the amount and the timing of cash flows.

T F   10. The most desirable investments are often those with the lowest net present values.

T F   11. Over its entire life, an investment with a net present value of zero will have a net cash flow of zero.

T F   12. Two investment proposals of equal cost are expected to generate equal net cash flows both in timing and amount. Of the two investments the one with the highest degree of risk will have the lowest net present value.

T F   13. All capital investment proposals with positive net present values should be approved if funding is available.

T F   14. In deciding whether to replace old equipment, two important considerations are: (a) the cost of the new equipment, and (b) the cost of the old equipment.

Completion Statements

Fill in the necessary word to complete the following statements:

1. The process of planning and evaluating investments in plant assets is called
_____ _____.

2. The length of time necessary to recover the entire cost of an investment from its annual net cash flow is referred to as the _____ _____.

3. The _____ ___ _____ _____ is the average annual net income from an investment expressed as a percentage of the average amount invested.

4. Discounting is the process by which the _____ _____ of cash flow is determined.

5. In determining an investment's present value, the _____ _____ may be viewed as the investor's required rate of return.

6. A(an) _____ net present value means that the investment is expected to yield a return greater than the discount rate, whereas a(an) _____ net present value means that the investment is expected to yield a return less than the discount rate.

7. The book value of a plant asset is considered a _____ _____ and is not relevant in capital budgeting decisions.

8. Determining whether an investment proposal is acceptable requires an analysis of the investment's _____ costs, revenue and cash flows.

Multiple Choice

Choose the best answer for each of the following questions and enter the identifying letter in the space provided.

___ 1. Which of the following is *not* a capital budgeting decision?
  a. The decision to build a new finished goods warehouse.

  b. The decision to lease or buy a new fleet of trucks.

  c. The decision to scrap or rebuild a batch of defective products.

  d. The decision to automate a manufacturing process with robotics.

___ 2. Which of the following is an example of a nonfinancial consideration in capital budgeting?
  a. Will the investment in a new machine improve employee morale?

  b. Will the investment in a new machine generate adequate cash flows to recover its cost in 3 years?

  c. Will the investment in a new machine generate an average return on investment greater than 12%?

  d. Will the investment in a new machine have a positive net present value?

___ 3. Which of the following is considered in the computation of an investment's payback period?
  a. The profitability of the investment over its entire life.

  b. The time an investor must wait before all cash flows are received.

  c. The minimum rate of return required by the investor.

  d. The investment's estimated annual net cash flow.

___ 4. Which of the following is *not* considered in the computation of the return on average investment?
  a. The profitability of the investment over its entire life.

  b. The average amount invested.

  c. The investment's estimated salvage value.

  d. The appropriate discount rate.

___ 5. The process by which the present value of cash flows is determined is called:
  a. Discounting.

  b. An annuity.

  c. Incremental analysis.

  d. Capital budgeting.

_ 6.   Which of the following does *not* affect the net present value of an investment proposal?

      a.   The method of depreciation used for financial accounting purposes.

      b.   The timing of future cash flows.

      c.   The cost of the investment.

      d.   The method of depreciation used for tax purposes

_ 7.   As the relative risk associated with an investment proposal increases:

      a.   The discount rate used to determine its net present value is decreased.

      b.   The net present value of the investment increases.

      c.   The minimum acceptable rate of return associated with the investment increases.

      d.   The average cost of the investment increases.

Exercises

1.   Listed below are eight technical accounting terms emphasized in this chapter.

Capital budgeting	*Return on average investment*
Payback period	*Average investment*
Discounting	*Incremental cash flows*
Annuity	*Net present value*

Each of the following statements may (or may not) describe one of these technical terms. In the space provided below each statement, indicate the accounting term described, or answer "None" if the statement does not correctly describe any of the terms.

a.   A uniform stream of cash flows to be received over time.

_____

b.   The process used to plan and evaluate investments in plant assets.

_____

c.   The length of time necessary to recover the entire cost of an investment.

_____

d.   A proposal's average annual income projection expressed as a percentage of the average amount invested.

_____

e.   One-half of the sum of an investment's cost plus its salvage value.

_____

f.   The process of determining the present value of future cash flows.

_____

g. The amount an investor should be willing to pay today in order to receive a specified amount of cash at some future date.

_____

2. The air conditioning system at Monic Corporation's assembly plant has been malfunctioning for several months. Based strictly on financial considerations, the company's accountant cannot justify investing in a new air conditioning system. What are some nonfinancial considerations that may justify investing in a new system?

3. Barker Corporation is planning to buy equipment to produce a new product. The equipment will cost $375,000 and have an estimated 10-year life with a $25,000 salvage value. Projected annual operating results from producing the new product as follows:

Incremental revenue $250,000
Incremental expenses
   Expenses other than deprecation 190,000
   Straight-line depreciation   35,000
Incremental net income ....$ 25,000

All revenue and expenses other than depreciation will be received or paid in cash. Compute the following for this proposal:

a. The annual net cash flow.

b. The payback period.

c. The return on average investment.

d. The net present value, using a discount rate of 10%. The present value of $1 due in 10 years discounted at 10% = .386. The present value of $1 to be received annually for 10 years discounted at 10% = 6.145.

SOLUTIONS TO CHAPTER 26 SELF-TEST

True or False

1. **F** Capital investments are generally long-term investments in plant and equipment. Thus, even well planned capital investments are difficult to reverse should economic conditions unexpectedly change.

2. **T** Most capital budgeting *techniques* involve only financial considerations. However, the *interpretation* of capital budgeting figures should include an analysis of nonfinancial considerations, including legal issues, ethical concerns, product quality expectations, etc.

3. **F** The average cost of an investment equals one-half of the sum of the original cost of the investment *plus* its salvage value.

4. **F** The payback period is the length of time required to recover the entire cost of an investment based on its annual net cash flows. The length of time required to do so is *not* divided by the investment's estimated useful life.

5. **T** The payback period ignores the total life of an investment and thus its total profitability. While the payback period is a useful analytical tool, it should not be the sole factor considered in making a capital investment decision.

6. **F** The return on average investment ignores the *timing* of an investment's future cash flows. While *earnings* are taken into consideration, no emphasis is placed on whether the *cash* receipts will occur early or late in the life of the investment.

7. **T** A cash amount received today can be invested to become the equivalent of a larger amount in the future.

8. **T** The present value of an amount of cash to be received 7 years from now is more than the present value of the same amount to be received in 10 years, as the amount of cash can be invested to earn a return for the 3 additional years.

9. **T** The discounted present value depends upon the amount of the future payment, the rate of return required, and the length of time until the cash flow will be received.

10. **F** The *least* desirable investments are often those with the lowest net present values. However, in some situations, even those investments with low net present values may be desirable when nonfinancial considerations are take into account.

11. **F** A net present value of zero results when the discounted present value of an investment's future net cash flows exactly equals the initial cost of the investment. A zero amount does not imply zero cash flows.

12. **T** Cash flows associated with the high-risk proposal will be discounted using a higher discount rate than the one used to discount the low-risk proposal. The higher discount rate will result in a lower net present value.

13. **F** From a strictly financial perspective, a positive net present value makes an investment potentially desirable. However, there may be important *nonfinancial* issues to consider that could make an investment undesirable, even if it has a positive net present value and funding is available.

14. **F** The cost of the old equipment is an example of a sunk cost and is therefore irrelevant to the decision process.

Completion Statements

1. Capital budgeting. 2. Payback period. 3. Return on average investment. 4. Present value. 5. Discount rate. 6. Positive, negative. 7. Sunk cost. 8. Incremental.

Multiple Choice

1. Answer **c**—the decision to scrap or rebuild a defective batch of products does not require a large investment in plant and equipment, nor does it have long-run implications. Thus, it is not considered a capital budgeting decision.

2. Answer **a**—employee morale is an important nonfinancial consideration. Payback period, average return on investment, and net present value are all financial considerations.

3. Answer **d**—the payback period ignores profitability over the life of an investment, the timing of cash flows, and the minimum rate of return required by the investor.

4. Answer **d**—the computation of the return on average investment does not take into consideration the present value of future cash flows. Thus, it does not require the use of a discount rate.

5. Answer **a**—discounting is the process used to compute the present value of an investment proposal's future cash flows.

6. Answer **a**—depreciation for accounting purposes is a noncash expense. As such, it does not affect the net present value of an investment. Depreciation for tax accounting does affect cash flow and, thus, the computation of net present value.

7. Answer **c**—as the relative risk of an investment proposal increases, the discount rate used to determine its net present value is **increased**, which implies that the minimum rate of return required by the investor has also increased. The increased discount rate results in a lower net present value and causes no change in the average cost of the investment.

Solutions to Exercises

1.
   a. Annuity
   b. Capital budgeting
   c. Payback period
   d. Return on average investment
   e. Average investment
   f. Discounting
   g. None (This statement describes the term present value.)

2. Ethical and legal responsibilities to provide a comfortable and safe work environment.
   Employee morale
   Increased worker productivity
   Lower employee turnover
   Less work-related sickness and fewer work-related accidents

3.
   a. $60,000 ($250,000 – $190,000)
   b. 6.25 years ($375,000 ÷ $60,000)
   c. 12.5% {$25,000 – [($375,000 + $25,000) ÷ 2]}
   d. Present value of annual cash flows
      ($60,000 x 6.145)............................ $368,700
      Present value of salvage value
      ($25,000 x .386)............................... 9,650
      Total present value.......................... $378,350
      Less: Cost of investment.................. 375,000
      Net present value of the proposal..... $ 3,350

HIGHLIGHTS OF THE APPENDIX

1.   In Appendix A, we present the selected financial statements of The Home Depot, Inc., a publicly owned corporation. Throughout the text we refer to elements of these statements. You should view this information as *reference material;* do not memorize it, but do learn how to ***locate information*** within it. The coverage of Appendix A in this Study Guide includes "Highlights" but no "Test Yourself" section.

2.   There are numerous elements to financial statements. The major ones are described briefly in the following paragraphs. These paragraphs follow the sequence in which these items appear in The Home Depot's financial statements.

3.   **Chairman's Letter** This is a letter to the stockholders from the company's chief executive officer. It tells you much about the company, but primarily the information that managements wants to make known. ***Management's Discussion,*** discussed below, contains similar information, but in more objective terms.

4.   **Consolidated Financial Statements** The Home Depot presents four general purpose financial statements discussed in this text. They include, (1) consolidated statements of earnings, (2) consolidated balance sheets, (3) consolidated statements of stockholders' equity and comprehensive income, and (4) consolidated statements of cash flows. These financial statements include the operating results and financial position of the company's subsidiaries. This is why they are referred to as "consolidated" statements. The balance sheets show the company's financial position at the beginning and at the end of the current year. The three other statements provide comparative figures for three consecutive years. Like most company's, The Home Depot uses a statement of stockholders' equity in lieu of a statement of retained earnings.

5.   **Note to Consolidated Financial Statements** These "notes" disclose information necessary for the proper ***interpretation*** of the financial statements. They should be viewed as an ***integral part*** of the company's financial statements. They, too, have been audited.

6.   **Management's Responsibility for Financial Statements** This short report describes management's responsibility for the financial information contained in the financial statements. Management is ***primarily*** responsible for the reliability and completeness of this information. The report is signed by the company's Chief Executive Officer, its Corporate Controller, and its Chief Financial Officer.

7.   **Independent Auditor's Report** In this section of the financial statements, an independent firm of Certified Public Accountants (CPAs) expresses an opinion as to the ***fairness*** of the financial statements contained in the financial statements. The firm has reviewed various other elements of the financial statements and considers them to be consistent with the information contained in the financial statements. ***KPMG LLP*** is The Home Depot's auditing firm.

8.   As stated earlier, we do not provide a "Test Yourself" section for Appendix A.

APPENDIX B
TIME-VALUE OF MONEY: FUTURE AMOUNTS AND PRESENT VALUES

HIGHLIGHTS OF THE APPENDIX

1. A very important consideration in investing is the concept of the time value of money. This concept is based on the idea that an amount of money received today has a present value that is always less than its future amount. This is because money on hand today can be invested to become equivalent to a larger *amount in the future*.

2. The difference between a future amount and its present value may be regarded as interest revenue (or expense) included in the future amount. The amount of the interest depends on two factors: (a) the rate of interest and (b) the length of time on which interest accumulates.

3. Typical applications of the time value of money include determining: (a) the amount to which an investment will accumulate over time, (b) the amount that must be invested every period to accumulate a required future amount, and (c) the present value of cash flows expected to occur in the future.

4. Table FA-1 in the text's appendix shows the amount to which $1 will accumulate over a given number of periods. By multiplying the factor from the table by the amount of the investment, the future amount of any present value can be calculated.

5. If the investor needs to determine how much to invest to accumulate a specified future value. The specified future value in Table FA-1 should be divided by the table value corresponding to the appropriate interest rate and the number of periods.

6. To accumulate a large future amount, an investor may make a periodic series of deposits. A periodic series of equal sized cash payments (or receipts) is called an *annuity*. Table FA-2 may be used to determine the future amount to which an annuity will accumulate. The future amount is determined by multiplying the factor from the table (corresponding to the appropriate interest rate and number of periods) by the amount of the periodic investments.

7. If the investor needs to determine the amount of the periodic investment needed to accumulate a specified future amount, the future amount is divided by the factor from Table FA-2.

8. The length of the period used to calculate the future value of an investment depends upon how often interest is earned (compounded). For example, if interest is earned monthly, a month is used as the period and the monthly interest rate is used.

9. The present value of an investment is the amount an investor would pay today for the right to receive an expected future amount of cash. The present value of a future amount depends upon (a) the estimated *amount* of the future cash receipt (or payment), (b) the *length of time* until the future amount will be received (or paid), and (c) the rate of return required by the investor. The required *rate of return* is called the discount rate and depends upon the amount of *risk* associated with the investment opportunity, and upon the return available from alternative investment opportunities.

10. Computing the present value of a future cash flow is called discounting the future amount. The easiest method of discounting a future amount is by the use of present value tables (Tables PV-1 and PV-2). Your textbook includes present value tables which show (a) the present value of a single, lump sum, amount to be received at a future date and (b) the present value of a series of equal-sized periodic cash flows, called an *annuity*.

11.   The use of present value tables can be demonstrated by finding the present value of $800 to be received annually for 10 years, discounted at an annual rate of 12%. Since this is a series of 10 *equal-sized* payments, Table PV-2 in the textbook is applicable. The present value of $1 received annually for 10 years, discounted at 12%, is 5.650, meaning $5.65. Therefore, the present value of the $800 annuity is $800 x 5.650, or **$4,520**.

12.   The interval between regular periodic cash flows is termed the **discount period**. Annual cash flows involve discount periods of one year; in these situations, the annual rate of interest is used as the discount rate. When the periodic cash flows occur on a more frequent basis, such as monthly, the discount rate must be expressed as a monthly interest rate. For example, an annual rate of 18% must be expressed as a monthly rate of 1.5% when the cash flows occur monthly. The discount rate must relate to the time interval of the **discount period**.

13.   The concept of present value has many applications in accounting, including the valuation of certain assets and liabilities, determining the portions of certain cash flows that represent payment or receipt of interest, and evaluating investment opportunities. Many of these applications are discussed below.

14.   Accountants use the term **financial instruments** to describe cash, equity investments in another business, and any contracts calling for the receipt or payment of cash. Examples include cash, accounts receivable, investments in marketable securities, and all common liabilities except for unearned revenue and deferred income taxes.

15.   Whenever the present value of a financial instrument **differs** significantly from the sum of the expected future cash flows, the financial instrument initially is recorded in the accounting records at its present value. Differences between this recorded present value and the actual future cash flows are accounted for as interest.

    Assume, for example, a company borrows $10,000 for one year, signing a $10,000, 9%, note payable. The cash outlay at the maturity date will be $10,900. But the note originally is recorded as a **$10,000** liability—an amount equal to its present value at the date of issuance. The other $900 will be treated as interest expense.

16.   In the preceding illustration, the terms of the note clearly distinguish between the principal amount (a present value) and interest. In other cases, however, the present value of the obligation must be **computed**.

17.   Consider, for example, **capital lease agreements** (capital leases are discussed in Chapter 10). When an asset is "sold" under a capital lease, the lessor records a receivable equal to the present value of the future lease payments, and the lessee records this present value as a liability. The present value of the future lease payments is computed by discounting these payments at a realistic interest rate.

18.   Companies sometimes issue notes payable which make no mention of an interest charge. The present value of such "non-interest-bearing" notes can be determined either by present value computations or, sometimes, by appraising the consideration received in exchange. If this present value is substantially **less** than the payments to be made on the note, the note should be recorded at its present value. The excess of the future payments over this **present value** will be treated as interest expense.

19.   Present values increase over time toward the actual amount of the future cash flow. Also, present values may fluctuate because of changes in the market interest rate, which is used as the discount rate. The present value of a financial instrument at a particular date after its issuance is called its **current value**.

20.   Some financial instruments (cash, investments in marketable securities, and postretirement obligations) **are adjusted to their current value** at the end of each accounting period. For other

financial instruments, the current value should be **disclosed** if it differs significantly from the carrying value shown in the financial statements.

Obligations for postretirement benefits are shown at the **estimated present value** of the future benefit payments earned by employees during the current and prior accounting periods. Because these benefits will be paid many years in the future, their present value is **much less** than the expected future outlays. (Accounting for postretirement costs is discussed in Chapter 10.)

21.   The only long-term liability **not** recorded in financial statements at its present value is deferred income taxes payable. This is because there is no "contract" determining the amount or payment date of deferred taxes. However, many accountants believe that deferred tax liabilities are overstated because they are not discounted to their present value.

TEST YOURSELF ON APPLICATIONS OF FUTURE AMOUNTS AND PRESENT VALUES

True or False

For each of the following statements, circle the T or the F to indicate whether the statement is true or false.

T   F   1.   The present value of an amount to be paid or received in the future is always less than the future amount.

T   F   2.   The future amount of an investment depends upon the interest rate and the number of periods on which the interest accumulates.

T   F   3.   Using a larger interest rate results in a larger future amount.

T   F   4.   The table of the "future value of $1 paid periodically for n periods" is used to compute the future amount of equal-sized or unequal-sized payments.

T   F   5.   As the number of periods increases the future value of an investment decreases.

T   F   6.   If an investment fund pays 12% interest compounded monthly for 5 years, the future amount should be determined using the factor for 5 periods at 12% interest.

T   F   7.   The discount rate used in computing the present value of a future cash receipt may be viewed as the investor's required rate of return.

T   F   8.   Using a higher discount rate results in a higher present value.

T   F   9.   The longer the length of time until a future amount will be received, the lower its present value.

T   F   10. The concept of present value is applicable to future cash receipts, but not to future cash payments.

T   F   11. All the factors in the table showing the present value of $1 to be received in n periods are less than 1.000.

T   F   12. The interest rate shown in a present value table must be interpreted as an annual rate, even if the time interval of the discount period is only a month.

T   F   13. Both accounts receivable and accounts payable are examples of financial instruments.

T   F   14. Financial instruments initially are recorded in the accounting records at present values whenever these present values differ substantially from the expected future cash receipts or outlays.

T   F   15. At every balance sheet date, the carrying values of all financial instruments are adjusted to their current values.

T   F   16. When the net present value of a proposed capital expenditure is zero, the proposal provides no return on investment.

T   F   17. When equipment is purchased in exchange for a "non-interest-bearing" installment note payable, the cost to be recorded is equal to the present value of the note.

T   F   18. The market price of a bond may be regarded as a present value, whereas the maturity value of the bond is a future value.

Completion Statements

Fill in the necessary word to complete the following statements:

1. The basic premise of the _____ _____ concept is that a dollar available today is worth (more, less) _____ than a dollar that will not be available until a future date.

2. The future amount of an investment depends on the_____ rate, and the period of time over which the _____ _____.

3. The _____ _____ of an amount of cash is always greater than its present value.

4. The process of determining the present value of a future cash receipt or payment is termed _____ the future cash flow.

5. The present value of a future cash flow depends upon three things: (a) the estimated _____ _____ of the future cash flow, (b) the _____ _____ _____ until the cash flow will occur, and (c) the _____ _____ used in computing the present value.

6. An annuity is a series of periodic cash flows that are _____ in dollar amount.

7. Present value tables may be used with discount periods of any length, but the _____ _____ must apply to the period of time represented by one discount period.

8.   Super Store borrowed $30,000 from First Bank by issuing a six-month note payable in the face amount of $31,200. At the date the loan is made, the present value of Super Store's liability to the bank is $_____; the difference between this amount and $31,200 represents _____ included in the face amount of the note.

9.   The market price of bonds may be regarded as the present value to bondholders of the future _____ and _____ payments to be received.

Multiple Choice

Choose the best answer for each of the following questions and enter the identifying letter in the space provided.

___ 1.   The present value concept is based on the premise that:

     a.   A cash flow that will not occur until a future date is equivalent to a smaller amount of money receivable or payable today.

     b.   The present value of a future cash flow is greater than the actual amount of the future cash flow, because money on hand today is more valuable than money due at a future date.

     c.   Money invested today can be expected to become equivalent to a smaller amount at a future date.

     d.   The present value of a future cash flow may be greater or smaller than the future amount, depending upon the discount rate.

___ 2.   The future value of a $100 investment that earns a 10% annual return for three years is:

     a. $110.00.

     b. $121.20.

     c. $133.10.

     d. $136.50.

___ 3.   Cipher Data Systems is required to accumulate $5 million in a bond sinking fund to retire bonds payable 10 years from now. Cipher will make annual equal payments to the fund at the end of each of the next 10 years. If Cipher can earn 12% annual return on the bond sinking fund, the required annual payments will be $284,916.52. If the return on the sinking fund is 10% instead of 12%, the required annual payments will be:

     a. $267,854.20.

     b. $275,453.55.

     c. $280,333.25.

     d. $313,735.33.

___ 4.   Assume that an investor has decided to invest $20,000 at the end of each of the next
5 years in an investment fund. If the investment fund earns 8% it will accumulate to
a total of $117,340. If the investment fund earns 10% instead of 8%, the
accumulated total amount will be:

    a. $111,430.

    b. $115,634.

    c. $116,450.

    d. $122,100.

___ 5.   Which of the following factors does not affect computation of the present value of a
future cash flow?

    a.   The discount rate.

    b.   The period of time until the future cash flow will occur.

    c.   Whether the future cash flow will be a cash payment or a cash receipt.

    d.   The dollar amount of future cash flow.

___ 6.   The present value of $121 due in two years, discounted at an annual rate of 10% is:
    a. $91.90.

    b. $96.80.

    c. $100.

    d. $110.

___ 7.   Wine Country Safari purchased a hot-air balloon on a contract requiring 24 monthly
payments of $730, with no mention of interest. An appropriate annual rate of interest
for financing the purchase of the balloon would be 12%. To determine the cost of
the balloon and the present value of the contract payable, Wine Country Safari
should discount:

    a. $730 for 24 periods at 12%.

    b. $17,520 for two periods at 12%.

    c. $730 for 24 periods at 1%.

    d. $17,520 for two periods at 6%.

___ 8.   The present value of $1,000 due in five years, discounted at an annual rate of 12%, is $567. If this $1,000 future amount had been discounted at an annual rate of 15%, the present value would have been:

    a. $497.

    b. $582.

    c. $621.

    d. $747.

___ 9.   The present value of $500 due in five years, discounted at an annual interest rate of 10% is $311. If the $500 is due in six years, rather than five, its present value would be approximately:

    a. $282.

    b. $311.

    c. $374.

    d. $500.

___ 10.   Present value techniques are not used to determine the financial statement valuation of:

    a.   Long-term notes payable with interest charges included in the face amount.

    b.   The long-term liability for deferred income taxes.

    c.   A long-term note payable with no stated interest rate.

    d.   The liability arising from entering into a long-term capital lease.

Exercises

1.   Listed below are seven technical accounting terms emphasized in this appendix:

Discount rate   *Present value table*
Annuity   *Discount period*
Present value   *Annuity table*
Future amount

Each of the following statements may (or may not) describe one of these technical terms. In the space provided below each statement, indicate the accounting term described, or answer "None" if the statement does not correctly describe any of the terms.

a.   The interval between regular periodic cash flows.

_____

b.   A table that shows the present value of $1 to be received periodically for a given number of periods.

_____

c.   An investor's required rate of return.

_____

d.   The amount that a knowledgeable investor would pay today to receive a certain amount in the future.

_____

e.   A series of equal-sized periodic cash flows.

_____

f.   The amount to which an investment is expected to accumulate.

_____

2.   Use the future value tables in your textbook to determine the future value of the following investments.

     a. $10,000 to be deposited today in a fund that earns 6% annually for 5 years.

     b. $1,000 deposited at the end of each of the next 3 years in a fund that earns a 8% annual return.

     c. $20,000 to be deposited today in a fund that earns 10% annual return for 4 years, compounded semiannually.

3.   Use the present value table in your textbook to determine the present value of the following cash flows:

     a. $10,000 to be received annually for seven years, discounted at an annual rate of 15%.

     b. $4,250 to be received today, assuming that money can be invested to earn an annual return of 12%.

     c. $400 to be paid monthly for 24 months, with an additional "balloon payment" of $10,000 at the end of the 24th month, discounted at a monthly interest rate of 1½%.

4.   On November 1, Airport Transport purchased a new van by making a cash down payment of $3,000 and issuing an installment note payable in the face amount of $12,000. The note is payable in 24 monthly installments of $500 each, beginning on December 1. The following statement appears at the bottom of the note payable: "The $12,000 face amount of this note includes interest charges computed at a rate of 1½% per month."

In the space provided below, prepare the journal entries needed on (a) November 1 to record the purchase of the van, and (b) December 1 to record the first $500 monthly payment and to recognize interest expense for one month by the effective interest method. (Round interest expense to the nearest dollar.)

General Journal			
Nov. 1	Vehicles		
Dec. 1			

SOLUTIONS TO APPENDIX B SELF-TEST

True or False

1.   **T** The amount by which the future cash receipt exceeds its present value represents interest.
2.   **T** The future amount depends on two factors (1) the interest rate and (2) the period of time.
3.   **T** As the interest rate increases, the future amount increases.
4.   **F** The table is used to find the future amount of a series of equal-sized payments only.
5.   **F** As the number of periods increase, the future amount increases.
6.   **F** The future amount should be determined by using the factor for 1% interest for 60 monthly periods.
7.   **T** Factors affecting the investor's required rate of return are the degree of risk associated with a particular investment, the investor's cost of capital, and the returns available from other investment opportunities.
8.   **F** The higher the discount rate used, the lower the present value.
9.   **T** Cash of $100 to be received in three years has smaller value today than $100 to be received next week.
10.   **F** The process of discounting cash flows applies to both cash receipts and cash payments.
11.   **T** The present value of an amount is always less than the future amount.
12.   **F** Present value tables can be used with discount periods of *any length*; the discount rate shown is the *rate per period*.

13. **T** The term *financial instruments* describes cash, equity investments in other businesses, and contracts calling for the receipt or payment of cash. This latter category includes both receivables and payables.

14. **T** The difference between this present value and the future cash flows is accounted for either as interest revenue or interest expense.

15. **F** The carrying values of *some* financial instruments (investments in marketable securities and liabilities for postretirement costs) are adjusted to their current values at each balance sheet date, but the carrying values of other financial instruments are not. For these other instruments, the current values usually are *disclosed* in notes accompanying the financial statements.

16. **F** When the net present value is zero, the proposed investment provides a rate of return equal to the rate used in discounting the cash flows.

17. **T** The negotiated purchase price is the present value of the note payable; part of each payment constitutes interest expense.

18. **T** The market price is the price investors are willing to pay today (present value) for the future *principal and interest payments*.

Completion Statements

1. Present value, more.   2. Interest, interest accumulates.   3. Future value.   4. Discounting. 5(a). Dollar amount, (b) length of time (or number of periods), (c) discount rate. 6. Uniform (or equal). 7. Discount rate. 8. $30,000; interest. 9. Principal (or maturity value), interest.

Multiple Choice

1. Answer **a**—a present value is always less than the future amount. Answers b and d are incorrect, because they both state that a present value is greater than the future amount. Answer c is incorrect because money invested today should earn interest and thereby become equivalent to a larger amount in the future.

2. Answer **c**—$100 x 1.10 x 1.10 x 1.10 = $133.10.

3. Answer **d**—$313,735.33. You need not compute this amount to answer the question. Use of a lower interest rate results in higher required payments. Only answer d is higher than the original required payments of $284,916.52.

4. Answer **d**—$122,100. You need not compute this amount to answer the question. The higher interest rate will result in a larger future amount. Only answer d is higher than the original future amount of $117,340.

5. Answer **c**—three factors involved in computing the present value of a future amount: (1) the size of the future amount, (2) the period of time until the future cash flow will occur, and (3) the discount rate. Whether the future amount is a cash receipt or a cash payment is not relevant.

6. Answer **c**—$121 ÷ 1.10 ÷ 1.10 = $100.

7. Answer **c**—the discount rate must relate to the discount period. As we are using *monthly* discount periods, we must state the interest rate as a monthly rate.

8. Answer **a**—$497. You need not compute this amount to answer the question. Use of a higher discount rate results in a lower present value. Only answer a is lower than the original present value of $567.

9. Answer **a**—$282. You need not compute this amount to answer the question. The longer the time until a future cash flow will occur, the smaller its present value. Only answer a is lower than the original present value of $311.

10. Answer **b**—the liability for deferred income taxes is the *only* long-term liability to which present value concepts are not applied. This obligation is not a *financial instrument*, because there is no

"contract" for payment. Tax laws may change at any time. Because of the uncertainty as to future tax rates and payment dates, no effort is made to reduce the deferred tax obligation to its present value. Many accountants believe that current practices can cause this liability to be substantially *overstated*.

Solutions to Exercises

1.
   a. Discount period
   b. Annuity table
   c. Discount rate
   d. Present value
   e. Annuity
   f. Future amount

2.
   a. $13,380 ($10,000 x 1.338)
   b. $3,246 ($1,000 x 3.246)
   c. $29,540 ($20,000 x 1.477) The appropriate factor is the one for eight 6-month periods at 5% interest.

3.
   a. $41,600 ($10,000 x 4.160)
   b. $4,250 (An amount received or paid today is stated at its present value.)
   c. Present value of $400 per month for 24 months, discounted at 1½% per month
   ($400 x 20.030) ....$ 8,012

   Present value of $10,000 due in 24 months, discounted at 1½% per month
   ($10,000 x .700) ....$ 7,000

   Total $15,012

4.

General Journal			
Nov. 1	Vehicles	13,015	
	Notes Payable		10,015
	Cash		3,000
	Purchased van paying part cash and issuing an installment		
	note payable with a present value of $10,015 ($500 monthly		
	payment for 24 months discounted at 1 ½% per month;		
	$500 x 20.030 = 10,015)		
Dec. 1	Notes Payable	350	
	Interest Expense	150	
	Cash		500
	To record monthly payment on installment note payable:		
	Payment		
	Interest ($10,015 x 1 ½%)		
	Reduction on principle		

HIGHLIGHTS OF THE CHAPTER

1. Three common forms of business organization found in the American economy are the *sole proprietorship,* the *partnership,* and the *corporation*. A sole proprietorship is any unincorporated business owned by one person. A partnership is an unincorporated business having two or more owners.

2. A sole proprietorship is any unincorporated business owned by one person. The principal characteristics of the sole proprietorship form of business organization include:

   a. Ease of formation.

   b. Ownership of business assets by the proprietor.

   c. Business pays no income taxes. The proprietor pays personal income taxes on business profits.

   d. Business pays no salary to the owner; the owner's compensation consists of the entire net income of the business.

   e. Unlimited liability. The owner is personally liable for all business debts.

3. In a sole proprietorship, a *Capital account* and a *Drawing account* are maintained in the ledger to show the equity of the owner. The Capital account is credited with the amount invested by the owner and with the net income earned by the business. The Capital account is debited when net losses are incurred. Withdrawals by the owner are debited to a Drawing account, which is closed into the Capital account at the end of the accounting period.

4. The income statement for a sole proprietorship does not include any salary expense for the owner or any income tax expense. The net income of a sole proprietorship must be sufficient to compensate the owner for: (1) personal services provided to the business, (2) capital invested, and (3) the degree of financial risk that the owner is taking.

5. Because the business assets of a sole proprietorship are owned by the proprietor, the assets may be freely transferred from the business. Therefore, the balance sheet of a sole proprietorship is less useful to creditors. In making a loan to a sole proprietorship, creditors carefully consider the solvency and credit rating of the *owner*, because the owner is ultimately liable for the debts of the business

6. A partnership is an unincorporated business having two or more owners. For accounting purposes, we view a partnership as an entity separate from the other activities of its owners. However, under the law, the partnership is not separate from its owners. The principal characteristics of a general partnership include:

   a. Ease of formation.

   b. Limited life. (A partnership is dissolved whenever there is a change in partners.)

   c. Mutual agency. (Each partner has the right to bind the partnership to a contract.)

   d. Unlimited liability. (Each partner may be personally liable for all the debts of the partnership.)

   e. Co-ownership of partnership property and profits.

   f. Partnerships pay no income taxes. Each partner pays personal income taxes on his or her share of partnership profits, regardless of the amount withdrawn from the business.

7. The most significant disadvantage of a general partnership is the unlimited liability of the partners for the debts of the partnership. Two special types of partnerships limit the personal liability of the partners: the limited partnership and the limited liability partnership.

8. A *limited partnership* has one or more general partners and also one or more limited partners. The *general partners* have the usual rights and obligations – they manage the partnership and have unlimited liability for the debts of the business. *Limited partners* are passive investors who do not participate actively in management of the business and are *not* personally liable for the debts of the partnership.

9. A *limited liability partnership* is a form of organization that is designed for professionals such as doctors, lawyers, and accountants. In this type of partnership, each partner has unlimited liability for his or her own professional activities, but not for the actions of other partners. Unlike a limited partnership, all of the partners in a limited liability partnership may participate in management of the firm.

10. Partnership accounting is similar to that for a sole proprietorship, except there are more owners. As a result, separate capital and drawing accounts are maintained for each partner. The *statement of partner's equity* shows separately the changes in each partner's capital account, including the amount of partnership net income or loss allocated to each partner.

11. The partnership agreement (contract) determines the amount of income or loss that is allocated to each partner. If no partnership agreement exists, state law generally provides for an equal split among the partners.

12. The net income of a partnership represents the partners' compensation for: (1) personal services to the partnership, (2) invested capital, and (3) assuming the risks of ownership.

13. The dominant form of business organization in the United States is the *corporation*. A corporation is a separate legal entity, having a continuous existence apart from its owners. Literally thousands, or even millions, of individuals may be the owners of a single corporation; thus the corporation is a ideal means of amassing large amounts of capital.

14. Ownership in a corporation is evidenced by transferable *shares of capital stock*, and owners are called *stockholders*.

15. A corporation offers certain advantages not found in other forms of business organizations:

    a. The liability of individual stockholders for the debts of a corporation is *limited to the amount of their investment*.

    b. Large amounts of capital may be gathered by issuing stock to many investors.

    c. Shares of stock are easily transferable.

    d. Corporations are often run by professional management. Stockholders do not have the right to intervene in the management of a corporation or to transact corporation business.

16. Some *disadvantages of the corporate form* of organization are:

    a. A corporation is a *taxable entity* and must pay a high rate of tax on its net income. In addition, the stockholders must pay personal income taxes on the dividends they receive. This taxation of corporate profits twice is often referred to as *double taxation.*

    b. Publicly held corporations are subject to a considerable degree of regulation and disclosure of their business and financial affairs.

    c. The separation of ownership and management may result in management practices which are detrimental to stockholders.

17. Regular corporations are subject to income taxes, which are levied as a percentage of taxable income. Taxable income is computed in conformity with income tax laws and regulations, not generally accepted accounting principles. Income taxes are recognized by a debit to Income Taxes Expense and a credit to a liability account, Income Taxes Payable.

18. The entry to recognize income taxes in an unprofitable period consists of a debit to Income Taxes Payable and a credit to Income Taxes Expense. "Negative" income taxes expense may be recorded if the corporation is able to recover some of the income taxes paid in profitable periods.

19. The stockholders of a corporation may not withdraw profits from the business at will. Instead, distributions of dividends to stockholders must be authorized by the board of directors. Cash dividends are stated at a specified amount per share. The amount received by each stockholders is proportional to the number of shares owned.

20. A dividend is declared by the board of directors on one date, and distributed on another. The journal entry to record the declaration of a dividend involves a debit to the Dividends account and a credit to a liability called Dividends Payable. To record payment of the dividend, the corporation debits Dividends Payable and credits the Cash account.

21. The owners' equity section of a corporation's balance sheet is called the *stockholders' equity* section. Stockholders' equity includes at least two classifications: (1) investment by the owner (*paid-in capital*), and earnings from profitable operations (*retained earnings*).

22. Retained earnings are increased by profitable operations and decreased by net losses and dividends. Therefore, the retained earnings of a corporation represents the cumulative net income (or net loss) of the business to date, less any amounts which have been distributed to the stockholders as dividends. Remember, retained earnings is an owners' equity account; *it is not an asset and is not a fund of cash.*

23. At year-end, the Income Summary account of a corporation is closed into the Retained Earnings account. This entry parallels the closing of the Income Summary account of a sole proprietorship into the owner's capital account. In addition, the Dividends account is closed to the Retained Earnings Account by debiting Retained Earnings and crediting Dividends.

24. When comparing net income of a corporation with that of an unincorporated business, it should be remembered that everyone who works for a corporation (including owners) receive a salary that is deducted in determining net income. In addition, the corporation pays income income taxes on its net income. Therefore, the net income compensates the stockholders only for the amount of their invested capital.

25. When extending credit to an *unincorporated* business, creditors often look to the solvency of the individual owners, because the owners often are personally responsible for the business debts. In extending credit to a *corporation*, the solvency of the business as illustrated by the corporate balance sheet is much more important. In small corporations, creditors will often ask for a personal *guarantee* of the loan by the major stockholders of the corporation.

26. An S Corporation is a special type of corporation that is taxed as if it were an unincorporated entity. S Corporation status is a most advantageous in the following situations:

    a. A profitable corporation plans to distribute most of its earnings as dividends. Thus, double taxation of profits is avoided.

    b. A new corporation is expected to incur net losses in its early years of operation. If the business is organized as an S Corporation, stockholders may deduct their "share" of net business losses in their personal income tax returns.

27. When an existing business (e.g ., a sole proprietorship or a partnership) is reorganized as a corporation, the corporation is a new business entity. The valuation of the corporation's assets and liabilities is based upon their *current market value* when the new entity is established, not upon their values in the accounting records of the old business.

28. When a partner contributes assets other than cash to a partnership, the valuations assigned to the noncash assets should be their *fair market values* at the date of transfer to the partnership.

29. The closing entries for a partnership are similar to those for a sole proprietorship. The Income Summary account is closed to the partners' capital accounts according to the profit-and-loss-

sharing agreement, and each individual partner's Drawing account is closed to that partner's Capital account.

30.   A *statement of partners' capital* shows the changes in each individual partner's capital account for the year. It starts with the beginning balance of the capital accounts, adds additional investments and net income, and subtracts net losses and withdrawals.

31.   Partnership profits and losses may be split among partners on a any basis agreed to by the partners. Often partnership contracts are designed to reflect the following factors:

    a.   The amount of time each partner devotes to the business.

    b.   The amount of capital invested by each partner.

    c.   Other contributions by each partner to the success of the firm.

32.   Profit-and-loss sharing agreements may be based on a fixed ratio, or they may provide for salary allowances to partners and/or interest allowances on partners' capital with the remaining profits divided in a fixed ratio.

33.   If the profit-and-loss-sharing agreement provides for salary and/or interest allowances and any *residual* profit or loss to be divided in some fixed ratio, these provisions are followed even if the net income for the year is less than the total of the salary and interest allowances. The excess of the salary and interest allowances over the net income is charged to the partners in the agreed residual profit-loss-sharing ratio. In some cases this may result in a particular partner being allocated a negative amount even though the partnership is profitable for the period.

34.   Salary and interest allowances to partners are merely a *step toward distributing net income*. These allowances are *not expenses* to be deducted from revenue in arriving at net income.

TEST YOURSELF ON FORMS OF BUSINESS ORGANIZATION

True or False

For each of the following statements, circle the T or the F to indicate whether the statement is true or false.

T   F   1.   The owner of a sole proprietorship is personally liable for all of the debts of the business.

T   F   2.   The major disadvantage of a sole proprietorship is a double taxation of business profits.

T   F   3.   Mutual agency means that each partner has the right to bind the partnership to contracts.

T   F   4.   In a general partnership, each partner's liability for losses is limited to his or her investment in the firm.

T   F   5.   In the absence of a specific agreement, the law generally requires that partnership profits be divided equally among the partners.

T   F   6.   A partner must pay personal income tax on the amount of withdrawals from a partnership, regardless of his or her share of partnership profits and losses.

T   F   7.   In a limited partnership, none of the partners has unlimited liability for the debts of the business.

T F 8. Limited partnerships are especially appropriate for firms of professionals such as doctors.

T F 9. In a limited liability partnership all partners generally participate in management of the firm.

T F 10. In evaluating the profitability of a partnership, consideration should be given to the fact that partners are not paid salaries for services to the partnership.

T F 11. Any stockholder of a corporation may personally be held liable for the debts of the corporation.

T F 12. A corporation has continuity of existence which permits the business to continue regardless of changes in ownership or the death of a stockholder.

T F 13. Stockholders do not make withdrawals from the business as do partners or sole proprietors but receive dividends instead.

T F 14. Cash dividends are declared by the board of directors, not by the stockholders of a corporation.

T F 15. If a corporation has a net loss, the loss will generally be increased by income taxes for the period.

T F 16. Retained earnings represent cash generated from profitable operations that has been retained in the business.

T F 17. The net income of a corporation must be sufficient to compensate stockholders for personal services provided to the corporation and invested capital.

T F 18. In determining whether to extend credit to a business, the balance sheet of a corporation would be more important to the lending decision than would the balance sheet of a sole proprietorship.

T F 19. The most appropriate form of business organization for a business that has a high risk of litigation is one that is unincorporated.

T F 20. When an existing business is incorporated, the assets are revalued to their fair market value on the date of incorporation.

T F 21. When a partner contributes noncash assets to a partnership, the assets should be valued at the amount the partner originally paid for the assets.

T F 22. When a profit-and-loss-sharing agreement provides for salary and interest allowances to the partners, these salary and interest allowances should be deducted from revenue in arriving at partnership net income.

T F 23. If a partnership has a net profit for a period, the allocation of profit to the partners will always result in an increase in the partner's capital accounts.

Completion Statements

Fill in the necessary word to complete the following statements:

1. From an accounting standpoint a sole proprietorship is treated as a separate _____ from the other activities of the owner. However, from a _____ standpoint the sole proprietorship and the owner are considered one and the same.

2. The large number of sole proprietorships existing in the United States probably results from the _____ _____ _____.

3. Income tax expense appears in the income statement of a _____ but does not appear in the income statement of a _____ _____ or a _____.

4. The right of each partner to bind the partnership to contracts is called _____ _____.

5. Ryan invested an additional $4,000 in partnership during Year 1. Her share of partnership net income for Year 1 was $9,000, of which she withdrew only $2,000. The amount of partnership income that Ryan must report on her individual income tax return is $_____.

6. A limited partnership has one or more _____ partners and one or more _____ partners.

7. The major disadvantage of a regular corporation is a concept referred to as _____ _____.

8. The most appropriate form of business organization for a firm of professionals is a _____ _____ _____.

9. The maximum possible loss of stockholder in a corporation is limited to _____ _____ _____ _____.

10. The two major sources of equity capital in a corporation are (a) the sale of _____ and (b) _____ earnings.

11 Carr and Davis agree to share profits in a 2 to 1 ratio after allowing salaries of $30,000 to Carr and $42,000 to Davis. Assuming that they earn only $18,000 before taking into account the salary allowances, Carr's share of the net income will be $_____ and Davis's share will be $_____.

Multiple Choice

Choose the best answer for each of the following questions and enter the identifying letter in the space provided.

___ 1.   Which of the following is *not* a characteristic is a sole proprietorship?
   a.   Unlimited liability.

   b.   Limited life.

   c.   Ease of formation.

   d.   Separate legal entity.

___ 2.   Which of the following is *not* a characteristic of a general partnership?
   a.   Limited liability.

   b.   Mutual agency.

   c.   Limited life.

   d.   Ease of formation.

___ 3.   An advantage of the partnership as a form of business organization would be:
   a.   Partners do not pay income taxes on partnership income.

   b.   A partnership is bound by the acts of the partners.

   c.   A partnership can be created without any legal formalities.

   d.   A partnership may be ended by the death or withdrawal of a partner.

___ 4.   All of the following are true for both general and limited partnerships *except:*
   a.   Both must have at least two partners.

   b.   All partners have the right to participate in the profits of the business.

   c.   All partners are liable for all debts of the firm.

   d.   Neither types are legal entities.

___ 5.   Which of the following are considered to be the most important disadvantages of general partnership as a form of business organization?
   a.   Limited life and double taxation.

   b.   Regulation and unlimited liability.

   c.   Unlimited liability and mutual agency.

   d.   Limited life and mutual agency.

___ 6.   Periodic withdrawals by partners are best viewed as:
   a.   Payment for partner's personal services to the partnership.

   b.   Expense of doing business.

   c.   Taxable income to the partners.

   d.   Distribution of partnership assets to the partners.

___ 7. Which of the following is **not** a characteristic of the corporate form of organization?

    a. Limited liability of stockholders.

    b. Mutual agency.

    c. Centralized authority.

    d. continuous existence.

___ 8. Title to the assets of a corporation is legally held by:

    a. The stockholders, jointly and severally.

    b. The corporation, as a legal entity.

    c. The president of the corporation in trust for the stockholders.

    d. The board of directors, as trustees.

___ 9. Which of the following is probably the most appropriate form of business organization for a large manufacturing company?

    a. A regular corporation.

    b. A general partnership.

    c. An S Corporation.

    d. A sole proprietorship.

___ 10. For which of the following types of organizations would a creditor consider the balance sheet of the business most important to making a lending decision?

    a. A sole proprietorship.

    b. A general partnership.

    c. A limited partnership.

    d. A corporation.

___ 11. Which of the following best describes the nature of salary and interest allowances in a partnership profit-and-loss-sharing agreement?

    a. Expense of the business, which should be deducted from revenue in determining net income.

    b. The amount upon which each partner will have to pay personal income tax.

    c. A means of allocating net income in relation to services rendered and capital invested by partners.

    d. A means of determining reasonable monthly withdrawals by each partner.

___ 12. Smith invests in a partnership some land which cost his father $10,000. The land had a market value of $15,000 when Smith inherited it six years ago, and currently the land is independently appraised at $25,000 even though Smith insists that he "wouldn't take $50,000 for it." The land should be recorded in the accounts of the partnership at:

    a. $10,000.

    b. $15,000.

    c. $25,000.

    d. $50,000.

Exercises

1. Listed below are eight technical accounting terms emphasized in this chapter.

Drawing account   *Corporation*
Retained earnings   *General partners*
Stockholders   *Limited liability*
Limited partners   *partnership*
Partnership contract

Each of the following statements may (or may not) describe one of these technical terms. In the space provided below each statement, indicate the accounting term described, or answer "None" if the statement does not correctly describe any of the terms.

a. A form of business organization that may hold legal title to business assets.

   _____

b. Owners of an unincorporated business whose liability for business debts is limited to the amount of their investments.

   _____

c. Owners of a business who have unlimited liability for the debts of the business.

   _____

d. A type of business organization that is particularly appropriate for a firm of professionals.

   _____

e. Capital of a corporation that results from investment by the owners.

   _____

f. An agreement among partners on the form and operations of a partnership.

   _____

g. An account that is used to record withdrawals of cash by an owner of an unincorporated business.

   _____

2. Listed below are descriptions of the major forms of business organization. In the spaces provided, indicate the letter of the form of business organization that is described.

   _____ An entity with a single owner who has unlimited liability for the debts of the business.

   _____ An entity that pays taxes on its business profits.

   _____ An entity with some, but not all, owners who have limited liability for the debts of the business.

   _____ An entity with multiple owners, all of whom are personally liable for all the debts of the business.

_____ An entity that does not pay income taxes on business profits with owners all of whom have liability limited to the amounts they have invested.

a Corporation
b Limited partnership
c S Corporation
d Limited liability partnership
e Sole proprietorship
f General partnership

3. K and L are partners in a business who share profits equally. Selected account balances are shown at the end of 20__.

Account	Amount
Income Summary	$24,000 (Cr)
K, Drawing	12,000 (Dr)
L, Drawing	15,000 (Dr)
K, Capital	50,000 (Cr)
L, Capital	75,000 (Cr)

a Calculate the amount of income from the partnership that K and L must report on their individual income tax returns.

K $_____   L $_____

b Complete the partially filled-in-statement of the partners' capital shown for the 20__, assuming that the partners did not invest additional capital in the business during the year.

K & L
Statement of Partners' Capital
For the Year Ended December 31, 20__

	K	L	Total
Balance, beginning of year...............	$50,000	$75,000	$125,000
Add: Net income for year.................	_____	_____	_____
Subtotal	$_____	$_____	$_____
Less: Withdrawals............................	_____	_____	_____
Balance, end of year.........................	$_____	$_____	$_____

4.   A and B are partners, having capital balances at the beginning of the current year of $20,000 and $30,000, respectively. Indicate in the appropriate columns the division of partnership net income between the partners under the specified conditions. If in any case the division results in a deduction from partner's capital, place parentheses around your answer to indicate this.

Transactions	A's Share	B's Share
First Situation: Net income of the partnership is $120,000; partnership agreement provides for:..		
a. Net income to be divided in the ratio of beginning capitals	$_____	$_____
b. Interest on beginning capitals at 12%; residual profit or loss divided 70% to A, 40% to B................	$_____	$_____
c. Interest on beginning capitals at 12% salary to A of $48,000, to B of $36,000, residual profit or loss divided equally........	$_____	$_____
Second Situation: Net loss of the partnership is $16,000; partnership agreement:		
a. Is silent as to sharing profits or losses..............	$_____	$_____
b. Provides salary to A of $28,000; salary to B of $20,000; residual profit or loss divided 40% to A and 60% to B	$_____	$_____

SOLUTIONS TO APPENDIX C SELF-TEST

True or False

1.   **T** A sole proprietor is personally responsible for all business debts.

2.   **F** The profits of a sole proprietorship are taxed only to the owner. Double taxation is a major disadvantage of a corporation.

3.   **T** Each partner acts as an agent of the partnership with authority to enter into contracts. Mutual agency means the partnership is bound by the acts of partners acting within the normal scope of operations.

4.   **F** Each partner in a traditional partnership is personally responsible for all debts of the business.

5.   **T** State laws generally provide that profits are equally split in the absence of a specific agreement.

6.   **F** A partner must pay taxes on his or her share of net income of the partnership, regardless of how much is withdrawn.

7.   **F** In a limited partnership, the general partners have unlimited liability for the debts of the partnership.

8.   **F** Limited partnerships are not appropriate for firms of professionals because the limited partners generally do not participate in the business. Limited partnerships are more appropriate for situations in which some "partners" actually are passive investors.

9. **T** In a limited liability partnership, all partners generally participate in the management of the business. This makes this form of organization especially appropriate for a firm of professionals.

10. **T** A partner's share of net income from the partnership must be adequate to compensate the partner for invested capital, services provided to the business, and the risks of ownership. Payments to partners for services provided are not an expense of the partnership.

11. **F** Stockholders of a corporation have limited liability for the debts of the corporation. They may lose only their investment.

12. **T** A corporation is a legal entity separate and apart from the owners. Changes in ownership do not affect the operations of the business.

13. **T** Distributions to stockholders of a corporation take the form of dividends.

14. **T** Dividends are declared by the board of directors who are elected by the stockholders.

15. **F** When a corporation has a loss for a period, it can often record negative income taxes which *reduce* the amount of the loss. Negative income taxes reflect the fact the corporation may obtain a refund of income taxes paid in profitable periods.

16. **F** Retained earnings represents capital that has been accumulated through profitable operations. However, it may be in the form of assets other than cash.

17. **F** If a stockholder provides services to a corporation as an employee or officer, the stockholder is paid a salary. This salary is deducted in determining net income of the corporation.

18. **T** In deciding whether to lend money to a corporation, a lender must rely on the corporation to repay the loan. The stockholders are not personally liable for the debts of the business.

19. **F** A corporation is a more appropriate form of organization for a business with a high risk of litigation, because the owners have limited liability for the debts of the business.

20. **T** When a business is incorporated, the assets are recorded on the corporation's books at their fair market values.

21. **F** When a partner contributes noncash assets to a partnership, the assets should be valued at their fair market values.

22. **F** The salary and interest allowances are used to determine how net income of the partnership is allocated among the partners.

23. **F** Salary and interest allowances may cause a partner's capital account to decrease in a particular period even though the partnership is profitable for the period.

Completion Statements

1. entity, legal. 2. ease of formation. 3. corporation, sole proprietorship, partnership. 4. mutual agency. 5. $9,000. 6. general, limited. 7. double taxation. 8. limited liability partnership. 9. the stockholders' original investment. 10. (a) stock, (b) retained. 11. $(6,000), $24,000

Multiple Choice

1. Answer **d** – a sole proprietorship is not a separate legal entity. It is an extension of the owner.

2. Answer **a** –the partners of a partnership have unlimited liability for the debts of the partnership.

3. Answer **c** – ease of formation is a major advantage of a partnership. The other items generally represent disadvantages of a partnership.

4. Answer **c** – in a limited partnership, the limited partners are not personally liable for the debts of the partnership.

5. Answer **c** – the most significant disadvantages of a general partnership are that other partners may bind the partnership to contracts and all partners are liable for the debts of the partnership.

6. Answer **d** – withdrawals, represent distributions of partnership assets to the partners.

7.   Answer **b** – mutual agency is a characteristic of partnerships, not corporation.

8.   Answer **b** – title assets of a corporation are held by the corporation. A corporation is a legal entity.

9.   Answer **a** – a manufacturing company generally needs large amounts of capital that can be best accumulated by a regular corporation.

10.   Answer **d** – a corporation is the only type of business organization that is solely responsible for the payment of its own debts.

11.   Answer **c** – salary and interest allowances are used to determine an allocation of net income that fairly compensates partners.

12.   Answer **c**– the land should be recorded at its fair market value on the date it was contributed to the partnership.

Solutions to Exercises

1.

     a.   Corporation
     b.   Limited partners
     c.   General partners
     d.   Limited liability partnership
     e.   None (This statement describes *capital stock*.)
     f.   Partnership contract
     g.   Drawing account

2.

     <u>e</u>   An entity with a single owner who has unlimited liability for the debts of the business.
     <u>a</u>   An entity that pays taxes on its business profits.
     <u>b</u>   An entity with some, but not all, owners who have limited liability for the debts of the business.
     <u>f</u>   An entity with multiple owners, all of whom are personally liable for all the debts of the business.
     <u>c</u>   An entity that does not pay income taxes on business profits with owners all of whom have liability limited to the amounts they have invested.

3.   a.   K <u>$12,000</u> ($24,000/2)   L <u>$12,000</u> ($24,000/2)

     b.

K & L
Statement of Partners' Capital
For the Year Ended December 31, 20__

	K	L	Total
Balance, beginning of year	$50,000	$75,000	$125,000
Add: Net income for year	12,000	12,000	24,000
Substotal..................................	$62,000	$87,000	$149,000
Less: Withdrawals	(12,000)	(15,000)	(27,000)
Balance, end of year	$50,000	$72,000	$122,000

4.

Transactions	A's Share	B's Share
First situation:	a $48,000	$ 72,000
	b $82,000	37,800
	c $65,400	$ 54,600
Second situation:	a $ (8,000)	$ (8,000)
	b $ 2,400	$(18,400)